WordPress Domination: Beginner to Ninja in 7 Days

 **W9-BVL-682**

Disclaimer:

Every effort has been made to assure that our books and reports are as accurate as possible. However, there may be typographical and content errors. This content should be used as a general guide and not as the solution.

The author and publisher shall have neither liability nor responsibility to any person or entity with respect to any loss, damage, or alleged to be caused directly or indirectly by information provided in this report or book.

Introduction

Hello everyone, this is Lambert Klein and this time I'm bringing you the definitive WordPress guide that will turn you into a WordPress ninja in just 7 days. This guide is designed to take you by the hand and familiarize you with how to get set up on WordPress, how to enhance the basic WordPress setup, and how to monetize your site for maximum revenue. While this guide is perfect for beginners, it was also created to meet the needs of intermediate and advanced users.

One of the best things about using the WordPress platform is that it's incredibly easy to get started. An experienced user can have a site up and running in less than an hour. However, WordPress doesn't exactly come with an instruction manual, and many new users can end up feeling lost, or worse, spending hours and hours looking up YouTube tutorials on how to do the most basic of tasks. At the same time, intermediate and advanced users may have WordPress down to a science but might also have trouble effectively monetizing the site, beating Google's Panda update, and driving targeted traffic.

The good news is that regardless of your skill level this guide will be your WordPress instruction book and make sure that nothing is left to chance when it comes to fully optimizing your WordPress website. Whether you're an Internet marketer looking to make a full-time income online or just a person looking to start a blog for the fun of it, this guide will help you make it happen!

One thing that should also be mentioned is that this book is best read when sitting in front of your computer. A lot of the material goes into extensive detail about how WordPress works, how to configure domains/web hosting, and more. It really helps to actually be doing this at your computer as you read this guide so that you don't get lost.

Also worth mentioning is that while much of the content in this guide is very specific, some is more general. This is because factors such as what web hosting you're using, what theme you have installed, and what plugins you're using make it impossible to give step-by-step instructions for certain things. In cases such as these, I seek to give you a general understanding of the topic to get you started. However, you may need to look up resources using Google or tutorials on YouTube for your specific situation.

Once you're done reading the main part of this book, don't forget to check the Resources chapter at the end. There is some good stuff in there, including links to tutorial videos that help you with some of the more complicated tasks.

Now that you understand how this WordPress instruction manual works, let's jump right in and get started. Stick with this guide and in 7 days you will have a fully functional, completely optimized WordPress website that you can be proud of!

NOTE: This book has many images to help you understand everything. If your Kindle doesn't show the images in the quality you desire, you may want to read this on the "Kindle for PC" software. It's a free download from Amazon.

Grab it here: Kindle for PC
www.amazon.com/gp/kindle/pc

Day 1 – Getting a Domain Name

The first day of building your WordPress website is going to be one of the easiest. In fact, you won't be using WordPress at all today. What you're going to be doing is first learning the difference between WordPress.com and WordPress.org, two similar yet different platforms.

I'm also going to be showing you how to purchase a domain as well as the factors that go into determining the perfect domain name for your website. Choosing the right domain name is the first major SEO task that you will complete, and it is very important for making sure that your site ranks well in Google and other search engines.

Chapter 1: WordPress.com vs. WordPress.org

The reason the WordPress platform is so popular is that it allows you to create websites without having to learn complicated HTML and CSS code. Before WordPress you would have to spend months learning this complicated programming language if you wanted to build a site. Now, thanks to WordPress, you can have a site up and running with a few clicks of a mouse.

The very first thing you need to understand, if you are new to the WordPress platform, is that there are two different types of WordPress: WordPress.com and WordPress.org. While these two platforms are very similar in function, there are some **major** differences as far as what you're allowed to do on each of them. Let's take a look at each platform so you can figure out which one is best for you.

WordPress.com

WordPress.com is a website that allows you to create a blog using the WordPress platform. When you sign up you have several URL options, such as [your blog name].wordpress.com which is free and other domains such as .com, .me and more that you have to pay for. The free option is generally the most popular.

The blog will also be hosted on WordPress's servers for you, and there are paid and free options. With the free option you only get the blog, but with the paid option you get the following:

- Domain name and mapping (allows you to register a domain name of your choice)
- 10GB space upgrade (adds more storage space)
- No ads (your free blog will have ads on it so WordPress can make money)
- Custom design (allows you to customize your font and theme CSS)
- Video press (allows you to upload and play HD videos)

All of these paid options cost $99 per year total, although there are discounts available at times. Even with the domain name and mapping, your site will still be hosted on the servers at WordPress.com and you will still be subject to their terms of service. In other words, WordPress owns your website.

With the free variant you get many different themes to choose from, but you will be unable to upload your own themes. You will also not be able to edit the themes you choose from the gallery either. However, you will be able to add your own custom header.

In addition, WordPress will also have the right to display ads on your site. The good news is that the ads are very infrequent, and logged-in users won't see them. For a $29.99 annual fee you can have ads removed entirely, if you didn't choose the paid version that removes them automatically.

Another major downside to WordPress.com (if you're looking to make money on your site) is the fact that you are not allowed to have any third-party advertisements on it. While you can sell your own products (which is great if you're a Kindle author or something of that nature), WordPress.com simply isn't ideal for a strong marketing effort.

One odd notable exception to this rule, as stated in the WordPress.com terms of service (TOS), is that you can write your own movie and video game reviews and link people to Amazon.com.

In addition to affiliate blogs, other types of blogs that Wordpress does not allow are autoblogs, SEO blogs, and scraper blogs.

You also can't add plugins to your WordPress.com site. Plugins are special programs that you can add to WordPress.org that enhance your site in various ways. Some browser-based WordPress plugins, such as Zemanta, do work with WordPress.com because they don't have to be uploaded onto the site itself.

Here is a quick recap of the pros and cons of WordPress.com:

Pros

- Very easy to set up
- Don't have to learn HTML or CSS
- Great for blogging
- Basic variant is free
- Don't have to worry about buying hosting or a domain name

Cons

- Can't upload custom themes
- Advanced features and ad removal come with a yearly fee
- Can't sell affiliate products, advertising space, or post AdSense ads
- Can't use plugins
- No control over your hosting
- Can't sell the site

In the end WordPress.com is really only useful if you plan on blogging for the fun of it or if you run a service-based business online and just need a website as quickly as possible and for free. WordPress.com is **not** recommended for anyone who is serious about online business, with one of the top reasons being that SEO (search engine optimization) is discouraged on WordPress.com, and this will limit your traffic. Also, third- party advertising is not allowed, which limits your business model to selling only your own products. For those who are serious about making money online, WordPress.org is going to be your best choice.

WordPress.org

WordPress.org is, quite simply, the easiest way to create a website that is designed to make money. While it does take a bit more effort to set up, and there is a bit more of a learning curve involved, its advantages over WordPress.com are many.

One of the best things about WordPress.org is the level of customization available to you. You can choose from **many** pre-made themes that can be found across the Internet for free, such as Flexibility, or you can choose from one of the Wordpress-provided themes. You can even hire someone to create a custom theme for you or make one yourself if you have the talent for that. You can also go into the CSS and edit your themes.

Another huge benefit of using WordPress.org is the fact that you can use plugins. As previously mentioned, plugins are programs that you add onto your site that perform different functions. Some plugins filter spam, some make your site load faster, while others give you extra fonts. There are thousands of plugins available, and we'll get into which ones are the best for your site a bit later.

WordPress.org is also the preferred platform for website flipping. If you want to build a site, rank it high in the search engines, drive traffic, and produce a revenue stream so that you can sell it, WordPress.org is perfect for you. WordPress sites tend to sell very well because most people are familiar with them and how they work, as opposed to HTML sites.

There are many other ways to monetize a WordPress.org site. You can participate in affiliate programs, create autoblogs, create websites with curated content, post AdSense ads, sell ad space, and much more. Because you own the site and are hosting it on your own hosting service, you can do whatever you want when it comes to monetization.

Also, because your site isn't hosted on the WordPress.com servers, you're free to do as much SEO as you want. Not only that, SEO is very easy to do using WordPress, especially if you have the right plugins for it. Doing SEO will help to drive plenty of traffic to your site, which can help explode your revenue.

Here is a quick rundown of the pros and cons of WordPress.org:

Pros

- ⚜ Very easy to use once you learn how
- ⚜ Don't have to learn HTML or CSS
- ⚜ Have complete control over the site
- ⚜ Can sell the site
- ⚜ Can use SEO
- ⚜ Can use custom themes
- ⚜ Can edit themes
- ⚜ Access to thousands of plugins
- ⚜ Have control over hosting
- ⚜ Can monetize your site any way you want

Cons

- ⚜ Takes a bit longer to set up
- ⚜ More of a learning curve
- ⚜ Responsible for obtaining your own domain name and hosting

As you can tell, the pros drastically outweigh the cons. WordPress.org is functionally superior to WordPress.com in almost every way, making it the clear winner here unless you just want to be a casual blogger. Because of this, the remainder of this guide will focus on WordPress.org, how to set it up, optimize it, and monetize it. However, due to the similarities between WordPress.com and WordPress.org, much of the information in this guide about how to set up your site will be applicable to the WordPress.com platform as well.

Now that you understand the difference between the two WordPress platforms we can move on and get you set up. As mentioned before, you do have to purchase your own domain name for WordPress.org, and that will be your task for Day 1.

Chapter 2: Purchasing a Domain Name

The first step for getting started with WordPress is purchasing a domain name. This is incredibly easy and can be done in less than 5 minutes. However, there are some things to keep in mind before you rush out and buy a domain name. This is especially true if you plan to monetize your website.

Branding

The first thing you want to think about is branding. This is important whether you plan on monetizing your site or not. You want to pick a domain name that perfectly describes your website or blog and encapsulates what you're all about. Your domain name should also be something memorable and easy to spell.

An example of good branding would be a site that sells cat litter boxes and has the domain name "buycatlitterboxes.com." Just from hearing the URL you can tell exactly what the site is about.

An example of poor branding for this business would be "cat-tastic.com." Even if the product itself is named "cat-tastic" no one is going to have a clue what the site is about just by hearing the name. Another problem is that it is hard to remember how to spell, thanks to the hyphen. As a rule you should avoid hyphens and numbers (8, 3, 12, etc.) in domain names at all costs.

Also remember that domain names with two words are great, if you can find them. They tend to be worth much more than domain names with more words. The thing is, two-word domain names are incredibly rare these days, so you may not be able to find one suitable for your website. Don't worry about this too much; just get a three-word name. Generally speaking, the more words in your domain name, the less it will be worth if you want to sell it later. So keep that in mind.

Types of Domains

When it comes to the different types of domains, .com is king. This is simply because it is the most common, and by far the easiest to remember. If your site is "dogwalking.net" many people will not remember that it is a .net and go to "dogwalking.com" instead. As you can probably tell, this can cause a lot of lost traffic in some cases and is terrible from a branding standpoint.

Another problem with .net, .info, and other top-level domains is that if you create a custom email address using your domain, such as "jim@dogwalking.net," people will also forget the .net when emailing you and send their messages to "jim@dogwalking.com" instead. This can be a huge problem if you use that email address for customer service.

Perhaps the worst thing about a non .com domain name is that it just isn't worth as much as a .com. This is due to the reasons discussed above and simply because a .com is a powerful branding force. If you have a website that is a .net, don't expect it to sell for as much as a .com if you do decide to sell it.

In the end, just make sure you get a .com as your domain. Don't settle for anything else, even if the particular name you want is already taken. Change up the name you were thinking of a bit and keep searching until you find a .com that works for your site.

The SEO Factor

If you're creating your site to make money, you need to do some serious keyword research before you even begin brainstorming ideas for your domain name. This is because you want a domain name with a high amount of search volume but a relatively low amount of competition. While terms that fit these criteria can be hard to find, they do exist.

There are three main ways to do keyword research: estimation, testing, and analytics. Analytics can only be used to gather keyword research if you already have a site set up and analysts installed, so for now we'll concentrate on estimation and testing.

Estimation

Estimation is simply using a keyword research program, such as the Google AdWords Keyword Tool, to see how heavily searched keywords are. This is considered estimation because these tools are not 100% accurate. However, in many cases the tools can give you a good idea of what to expect in terms of traffic.

To use the Google AdWords Keyword Tool, simply go to https://adwords.google.com/o/KeywordTool. Type the keyword you're thinking of having in your domain name into the box and click "Search." You can also refine your search by selecting Broad, [Exact] and "Phrase" as needed. Here is an example of how that works using the keyword "dog walking."

Broad looks like this when someone types your keyword into Google:

Walking the dog
dog walking classes
dog obedience walking

As you can see, the keyword can be split, as long as it appears.

[Exact] looks like this in Google:

dog walking

This is the exact keyword with no other words added.

"Phrase" looks like this:

dog walking classes
how to dog walking
tips on dog walking

In this case "Phrase" simply ensures that the keyword isn't split up.

While [Exact] is the most refined search option, it may not cover all instances of people searching for your keyword. This makes it better to choose "Phrase" for keyword research purposes in most cases, but once again be aware that the data isn't going to be 100% accurate.

Once you type in your keyword and get the results back, you will notice that not only do you get search data on your keyword, but also a list of other keyword ideas. Take note of these and see if any of them have a particularly high search volume.

You will also notice that search results are calculated for both local and global. If your site is advertising a service that only operates in a local area, such as hairstyling, you want to pay more attention to the local results. If you're selling digital products worldwide on your site, then the global results will be more important to you.

Keyword	Competition	Global Monthly Searches ?	Local Monthly Searches ?
"dog walking" ▾	Low	201,000	90,500
"dog walking rates" ▾	High	2,900	1,600
dog walking rates ▾	High	5,400	3,600
dog walking service ▾	High	18,100	8,100

Once you have found some keywords that have a good search volume, you can then begin checking your competition. You may notice that there is a section in Google AdWords Keyword Tool that says "competition." This is not the competing websites but rather how competitive the AdWords listing is for that term. This is pretty much irrelevant at this point but can give you an idea whether there is money to be made from your keywords, because a lucrative keyword will have plenty of AdWords ads targeting it.

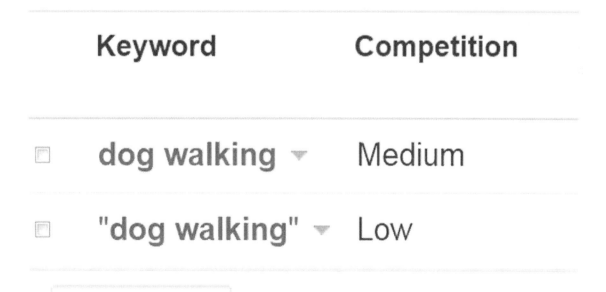

Keyword	Competition
dog walking ▾	Medium
"dog walking" ▾	Low

To estimate your competition go to Google.com and begin typing in your keywords to see what comes up. Once again you can use Broad, [Exact], or

"Phrase" to do these searches. While this is situational, in most cases it can be best to use "Phrase," which is simply your keyword in quotation marks.

Once you type your keyword in and do your search, take note of how many pages come up. Generally speaking, the fewer pages that come up, the easier it will be to rank for that keyword. However, the main factor determining whether or not you can rank on Page 1 for your keyword is the strength of the pages that are already on Page 1. There are ways to measure this, which we'll get into in just a moment.

dog walking	🔍

About 115,000,000 results (0.29 seconds)

Overall, the estimation method isn't perfect, but many people use it because it's free and can be done in a matter of minutes. The other method available to you right now, testing, is much more accurate but does have a few drawbacks.

Testing

If you absolutely demand accurate keyword data then you're going to want to do some actual testing, using Google AdWords because you want Google data. Google is the dominant search engine, after all, and will be responsible for the majority of your organic traffic. Of course, if you don't have a site yet then skip this for now.

To test the search volume of a keyword, you have to sign up for Google AdWords http://google.adwords.com/ and start a campaign. This isn't too complicated, and Google walks you through the process. What you're essentially going to do is run an ad for a day or two and measure the amount of clicks you get. Your ad will show up on the right side of Google searches and consist of a title and a short description.

About 549,000 results (0.30 seconds)

Ads related to gout triggers

What Causes Severe Gout? | TreatSevereGout.com
www.treatseveregout.com/
Learn How People Get Severe **Gout**, And Find a Treatment Option Now.

Gout Attack? | gout.com
www.gout.com/
Get Free Tips to Help Manage and Reduce Painful **Gout** Attacks.
What is Gout? - What Causes Gout? - Manage Your Gout.

✔ **9 Surprising Triggers of Gout Pain - Health.com**
www.health.com/health/gallery/0,,20458446,00.html
Got **gout**? Aspirin, hormones, dehydration, and other factors that can **trigger gout**

Why these ads?   Ads - Why these ads?

Gout Diet & Med Info
www.thegoutmed.com/
Discover a Prescription to Help
Manage the Root Cause of **Gout**.

What Causes The Gout
www.ask.com/What+Causes+The
Explore What **Causes** The **Gout**.
Satisfy Your Curiosity on Ask.com

Foods That Trigger Gout
www.lifescript.com/

Now, when you're doing this the most important part is to set your budget cap to between \$5 and \$10 a day, to keep you from running up a massive tab while doing this. Also, \$10 to \$20 should be more than enough data to tell whether or not a keyword is getting traffic.

Basically, you're going to add up the clicks your ad got and multiply that. So, if you got 60 clicks in one day you'd multiply that by 30 and get 3000, the amount of visitors you'd expect to get in a month.

Remember, there is a small margin of error when using this method due to two factors. The first is the fact that the more competitive keywords have a higher cost-per-click, and \$10 to \$20 may not cover enough clicks to get a lot of accurate data for you. This can be overcome by some simple mathematics. Let's say your budget for day one runs out and reaches \$10 in a 4-hour period. Take that amount and multiply it by 6 to get 24, and calculate what you would have gotten for the day. Now this isn't perfect, but it is close enough in most cases.

The second factor for margin of error is your ad itself. If you're awesome at writing ads you will get more clicks, which is fine. However, if you aren't any

17

good at writing ads you will get fewer clicks, which can skew your results. To compensate for this take time to learn some basic copywriting techniques related to writing AdSense ads. This is very simple and doesn't require a huge learning curve. Not only will this help you get more accurate results when doing keyword research, it will also help you understand how to write attractive titles for your website and web pages so that people click on them.

Also, another word of advice: Don't use the word "scam" in your ad when testing keywords unless it is actually part of your keyword itself. This is because the word "scam" is a very hot word that typically gets a ton of clicks. Using this when testing can really skew your results.

Overall this testing method isn't 100% perfect, but it is a vast improvement over the estimation method in terms of accuracy, because you are actually collecting real data. The only drawback is of course that it does take a bit of time and money to do these tests.

The second part of testing is to identify your competition. You will do this in exactly the same way as the estimation method, only you will take things a bit further using a tool known as SEOmoz Toolbar, which you can get by clicking here.
http://www.seomoz.org/seo-toolbar

With this tool you're going to go and look at all 10 websites on the first page of the search results for your keyword and analyze their statistics. You're going to look at the Page Authority (PA) and the Domain Authority (DA).

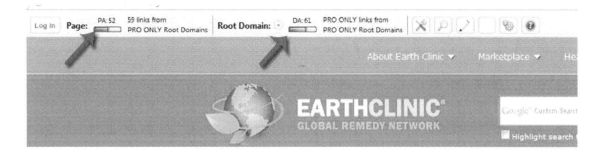

If two or more sites on Page 1 of Google have 40 or fewer in both of these categories, getting your website up onto Google Page 1 should be very easy. If you want, you can do this method before the AdWords test in order to ensure you don't spend money testing keywords that have extremely strong competition.

Regardless of whether you're using estimation or testing, you need to ultimately pick out several keywords that you like, that have a high search volume and low competition. Once you have this list of keywords that you'd possibly like to use in your domain name, it's time to move on to a registrar to purchase the name itself.

Choosing Your Registrar

When it comes to choosing which site to use to register your domain name, there are many options available. However, the two most popular registrars are Go Daddy and Namecheap. As far as price goes either one can be cheaper at any given time just depending on what discounts they happen to have available. Before purchasing a name at either place, do Google searches on "Go Daddy coupon code" and "Namecheap coupon code" to make sure you're getting the best discounts available.

An advantage that Go Daddy has over Namecheap is that more people use it. This means that if you ever sell your domain and/or site you can transfer the domain more easily if your customer is already signed up on Go Daddy.

Transferring domains between registrars isn't hard but does take a bit more of a learning curve to do.

Choosing the Right Domain Name

Regardless of what registrar you choose, the purchasing process is basically the same and starts with running a search for your desired URL. Once again I highly suggest you search for a .com.

Basically all you're going to do is type your most preferred keyword into the search box and see what comes up. If your keyword is only two words, don't expect to find it as a .com. Don't worry about this, just add another word to it.

For example, if your keyword is "dog training" and "dogtraining.com" is taken you can try "bestdogtraining," "dogtrainingclasses," "affordabledogtraining," and words like that. Keep in mind that if your site is going to be advertising a local business, adding a geo term can be really beneficial. Examples of that would be: "memphisdogtraining," "losangelesdogtraining," or "detroitdogtraining." This will help people in your area find you much easier.

Search	Customize	Checkout

DETROITDOGTRAINING.COM
is available. Just $12.99* `Add`

New search
More options

.COM	.CO	.INFO	.NET	.ORG	.WS	.US	.CA	.BIZ	.ME
Add	Add	Add	Add	Add	Add	Add	Add	Add	Add
$14.99* $12.99*	$29.99 $12.99	FREE with .COM or .CO	$14.99* $9.99*	$16.99* $6.99*	$14.99/yr	$19.99 $3.99	$12.99/yr	$14.99* $5.99*	$19.99 $9.99

Variations You Might Also Consider

Why should I register these?

	Domain	Price
Add	Detroit-Dog-Training.com	$14.99* $12.99*
Add	Michigan-Dog-Training.com	$14.99* $12.99*

Once you've done a few searches and have found an acceptable .com you can then go through the checkout process. Keep in mind that you will have to renew your domain every year unless you are on a plan in which it is registered for more than one year. You can set your subscription so that your bank account or credit card is billed automatically in most cases. Also, don't forget to use the promo code that gets you the biggest discount.

Also keep in mind that you can get something known as "whois guard" when you go through checkout. Whois guard basically protects your identity and allows you to register the site anonymously. It also typically costs a little extra. Whois guard can be beneficial in some cases but is ultimately up to you. Namecheap has been known to give free whois guard registration at times.

If you are a domain name investor, you should not get whois guard because it can prevent potential customers from being able to find your contact information. Domain investing is beyond the scope of this guide.

Once you are finished purchasing your domain name, it will show up in your control panel on your registrar's website. Sometimes this can take a few minutes, or even hours in some cases, after you make your purchase. You'll be accessing your domain name here later in order to point it to your server once you buy hosting, which is what you'll be doing on Day 2.

Day 1 Recap

Here is what we went over today:

- ⚖ The difference between WordPress.com and WordPress.org
- ⚖ The importance of brandable, high-search-volume keywords
- ⚖ Why .coms are the best top-level domains
- ⚖ How to find good keywords using Google AdWords Keyword Tool and the Google search engine (estimation)
- ⚖ How to find good keywords using Google AdWords and SEOmoz Toolbar (testing)

- How to register your domain name
- How to find promo codes
- What whois guard is and why you should consider it

Congratulations on completing Day 1! With an SEO-optimized, highly brandable domain name in your possession, you are well on your way to having an awesome WordPress website. Also, don't forget that domain name you just purchased is an asset with tangible value and should be viewed as such. Domain flipping and investment is an entire industry in and of itself, after all.

Day 2 – Getting Web Hosting

Now that you've chosen a domain name that is both SEO friendly and brandable, you're going to have to purchase hosting, which is essential for WordPress.org based sites. Web hosting is basically renting a web server to host your actual site data on. Alternately, you could purchase your own physical servers, but that would be both expensive and impractical for our purposes.

Today we're going to go over how to purchase hosting, which hosting companies are the most popular, setting your nameservers, and getting WordPress set up on your domain and on your hosting server. This will be a bit more challenging than Day 1, but overall this is pretty simple stuff.

Chapter 3: Purchasing Hosting

There are many different hosting companies to choose from, and you may be overwhelmed at first. It would be impossible for this guide to cover them all, so we'll just be taking a look at two of the most popular, Bluehost and HostGator. These services have a lot in common, but there are a few differences worth noting. Let's see what Bluehost has to offer first.

Bluehost

Bluehost is a great hosting service and one I use personally. It has everything you need to run a WordPress site easily and efficiently. There are two basic plans you can sign up for, Regular and Reseller. Reseller hosting comes in three different varieties on Bluehost and allows you to rent server space to others as a reseller of Bluehost web hosting. Because this isn't really the focus of this guide, we'll just go over Regular hosting.

Regular hosting on Bluehost only comes in one variety (unlike HostGator), but it does have everything you need to create an impressive WordPress site. Here are some of the notable features you get when you purchase Regular hosting.

- 24/7 U.S.-based customer support
- 1-click installs for many programs
- Unlimited disk storage
- Unlimited domain hosting
- Supports international domains
- 3 different web mail solutions
- Unlimited GB of site transfer
- Unlimited add-on domains
- Unlimited parked domains
- Courtesy site backups

- cPanel account control panel
- FTP access

To view the complete list click here.
http://www.bluehost.com/cgi/info/hosting_features

Bluehost is also very affordable and is usually $7.95 a month, although there are discounts at times. Also, there are promo codes that you can use for even more discounts. Don't forget to search Google for "Bluehost promo code" before signing up if you decide to go with Bluehost.

Overall Bluehost is a great service for beginners and more experienced users alike when it comes to web hosting. Bluehost also makes installing WordPress extremely easy, as I'll show you in just a little bit. First, let's take a look at the other hugely popular hosting service, HostGator.

HostGator

Like Bluehost, HostGator is an incredibly easy-to-use web hosting service. One notable difference between the two is the fact that HostGator has more plans to choose from, allowing you to pick what you need instead of simply giving you a "one-size-fits-all" plan. Here are some of the different plans available at HostGator.

Hatchling Plan
- Single domain hosting
- Unlimited disk space
- Unlimited bandwidth
- $8.95/month

Baby Plan
- Unlimited domain hosting
- Unlimited disk space

- Unlimited bandwidth
- $9.95/month

Business Plan

- Unlimited domain hosting
- Unlimited disk space
- Unlimited bandwidth
- Free private SSL and SP
- Free toll-free phone number
- $14.95/month

For creating a WordPress site I recommend the Baby Plan, in case you want to add more domains in the future. If you want, you can just get the Hatchling Plan and upgrade to the Baby Plan later if you really don't need unlimited domains right now. You probably also noticed that HostGator prices are a bit higher than Bluehost. While this is true, you can get discounts for your first month and use promo codes as well.

One advantage that HostGator has in the area of price is its "penny hosting" discount. You can obtain this discount by using the promo code 404PAGE. This code subtracts $9.94 from your first month and will get you the Baby Plan for $0.01 and the Hatchling Plan for free. The Business Plan becomes $5.01 for the first month. This discount is great if you're on a shoestring budget and need a bit of time to get your website up and running to make some money.

There is also Reseller hosting on HostGator that comes in five different varieties as well as VSP Hosting and Dedicated Server plans. Because these aren't really important for this guide we won't go over them. Before we move on, let's take a look at some of the features that all standard HostGator plans share.

- 24/7 support
- Instant data backups

- ↟ No contract
- ↟ 99.9% uptime guaranteed
- ↟ Unlimited add-on domains (not available for Hatchling)
- ↟ Unlimited parked domains (not available for Hatchling)
- ↟ Sub domains
- ↟ Free module installation
- ↟ Email alias
- ↟ Autoresponders
- ↟ Mailing lists
- ↟ Email forwarding
- ↟ Latest cPanel
- ↟ Instant forums
- ↟ Instant guestbook
- ↟ 3 email clients
- ↟ Free Google AdWords $100 credits

To view the complete list <u>click here</u>, http://www.hostgator.com/shared.shtml then click where it says "Compare All Hosting Plans."

I also want to take a moment to explain that last benefit on the bulleted list, the Google AdWords credits. Something really cool about HostGator is that occasionally in the mail you will receive free $100 credits for Google AdWords. These can be used to test out keyword search volume, as we discussed earlier, or to drive traffic to your website once you have it up and running.

Choosing the Right Hosting

As you can tell, both Bluehost and HostGator have their own sets of benefits. While Bluehost is a bit cheaper, it does lack some of the features and plans that HostGator offers. In the end both services are amazing and make setting up and managing a WordPress site incredibly easy.

In the end, which service you sign up for is up to you, and don't forget that there are many other hosting services available in addition to HostGator and Bluehost. Make sure you search for promo codes and discounts regardless of which service you choose, and that the monthly payment plan is set up in a way that you're able to easily manage.

Click here to visit Bluehost.
http://www.bluehost.com/

Click here to visit HostGator.
http://www.hostgator.com/

Root Domains and Add-on domains

When you purchase hosting you will be prompted to enter a domain name in most cases and will even be offered a free domain sometimes, depending on which hosting company you sign up with. Something very important that you need to remember is that the domain name you sign up with to get web hosting is your root domain, and any domains you add later will be considered add-on domains.

There isn't a big difference between these, but the way you access your root domain is different from how you access add-on domains. This can be confusing when you're trying to upload files if you aren't familiar with it. Later, when we're discussing how to upload files, I will go over how to access each of these.

Chapter 4: Setting Nameservers

Once you have both hosting and a domain name, you will then have to set your nameservers so that your domain shows up on your hosting. In most cases this is incredibly easy and only takes a few minutes to do. In some cases your root domain will show up on your hosting server automatically if you purchased that domain (or got it for free) through your hosting company. All add-on domains will need to have their nameservers set, though.

The first step to setting your nameservers is to figure out what your nameservers are. Nameservers are two number/letter combinations that will be given to you in one of the first emails you're sent after signing up for hosting. If for some reason you can't find that email your nameservers should be located somewhere in your cPanel. Here is an example of what a typical nameserver looks like.

ns.123.hostgator.com
ns.124.hostgator.com

Of course the numbers will be different for you, but this is basically what nameservers look like. Once you have your nameservers it's time to go into the account you have with your registrar and type them into the designated area.

Go Daddy is known for their somewhat confusing interface that they tend to change a lot. Basically what you're going to do after logging in is click "My Account" and then "Account Summary." Find the domain you just purchased, and then click on it to bring up a new screen.

On the new screen click on "set nameservers" and you get a pop-up window. In this window select the button next to "I have specific nameservers for my domains" and enter your two nameservers in the first two boxes below.

34

Domain Information

Registered: 7/2/2011

Locked: Locked

Expires On: 7/2/2012

Auto Renew: On
Extended Auto Renew: Off

Status: Active

Authorization Code:

Forwarding: Off

Manage

Renew Now
ConsoliDate Now!

Manage
Get Extended Auto-Renew!

Refresh Page

Send by Email

Manage

Nameservers

Nameservers: (Last update 7/2/2011)
NS819.HOSTGATOR.COM
NS820.HOSTGATOR.COM

Set Nameservers
Manage DS Records

Set Nameservers

* Required

If you are hosting your Web site with us (you have a hosting account with us associated with this domain) or you want to Park or Forward your domain, we will automatically set your nameservers for you.

Did You Know?

Domains using our nameservers benefit from our worldwide DNS presence through Anycast DNS.
Learn More

○ I want to **park** my domains.
○ I want to **forward** my domains.
○ I have a **hosting account** with these domains.
◉ I have **specific nameservers** for my domains.

Nameserver 1: *	Nameserver 2: *	Nameserver 3:	Nameserver 4:
▮▮▮.COM	▮▮▮.COM		

Add more | Manage DS Records

OK Cancel

For Namecheap, log in and you will be taken to your user page. On the main page, just hover your mouse over the "My Account" tab, and then click where it says "Manage Domains." Now click your domain to open a new page.

On this new page click where it says "Domain Name Server Setup" on the left and the nameserver page will come up. Click the bubble that says "Specify Custom DNS Servers" then enter your nameservers in the first two boxes and save changes.

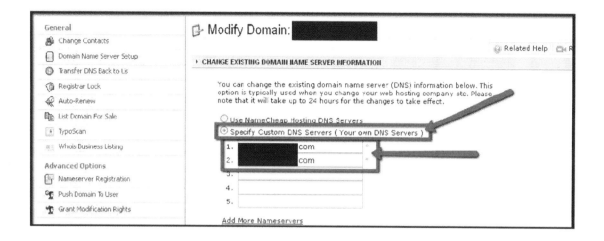

When setting nameservers it usually takes a few minutes for your domain to show up in your hosting cPanel. In some cases it can take up to 72 hours. If it takes longer than that, you should verify that you entered the nameservers correctly, and then contact customer support if you did.

Once your domain is showing up in your cPanel you can then install WordPress on it and begin building your website.

Chapter 5: Installing WordPress

Installing WordPress is going to be different depending on who you have web hosting with. In most cases, such as with Bluehost and HostGator, installing WordPress is incredibly simple and will take only a few minutes. There is some important information you need to be aware of when setting this up, such as your admin name and subdomain. I'll walk you through how to do this with Bluehost and HostGator.

Installing WordPress on Bluehost

To install WordPress on Bluehost simply sign in to your cPanel and scroll down to where it says "Software/Services" and click on the WordPress icon. This will bring up a new page where you simply need to click on "Install."

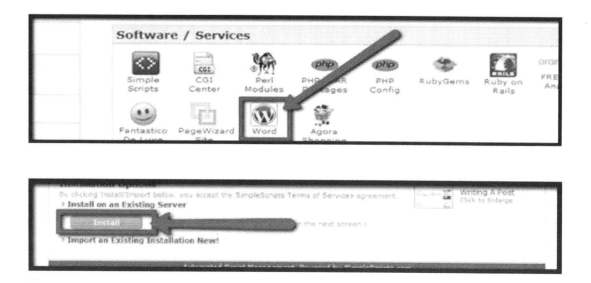

This will take you to another page where you must select the version of WordPress you want to install. Select the latest version. Now indicate where you want WordPress installed. The easiest way to do this is to leave this field blank and install WordPress on the root directory. If you want it in a subdirectory, type what you want to call it into the box.

For example, if your domain name is hockeyfans.com and you type in "database" WordPress will be installed on "hockeyfans.com/database." In most cases this is not recommended.

Once that is done go down to where it says "Advanced Options" and open up that section by clicking "Click here to display." Here you will enter the title of your site that you can change later if you want. This will appear in the header of your site for now.

You will also need to assign your username and password. Default username is "admin" but I recommend you change it to something else. Not only will you use your username and password to log in to your WordPress control panel, the username will also show up as the post author in some themes as well as in the comments section if you post there. For example, if your username is "admin" your name will show up simply as "admin." This is why you should choose something better than admin.

Something to keep in mind is the fact that your username that you log in with is permanent. However, you can change what is known as your "display name," the name that shows up on your site, later on. We'll discuss more about this a bit later, but for now just choose something you think sounds good.

Keep "Automatically create a new database" selected and then read the terms and conditions. Once you've done that check the box and then click "Complete."

Another page will now open up and WordPress will install. This takes only a few seconds, and once it is done you get a link to your site as well as a link to your WordPress control panel and your login information. Remember, you can always access your control panel by typing your URL followed by "/wp-admin." to bring up the login screen.

As you can see, installing WordPress on Bluehost is pretty easy. Here is how to install WordPress on HostGator.

Installing WordPress on HostGator

To install WordPress on HostGator, log in to your cPanel and scroll down to the icon that says "Fantastico De Luxe," which looks like a blue smiley face. Click that and you'll be taken to a new page.

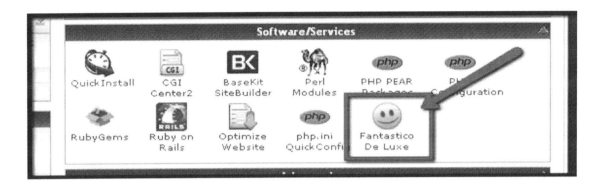

On this page check out the column on the left and click where it says WordPress, under "Blogs." A new section will open up on the right, and there will be a link that says "New Installation." Click that to move on to the next step.

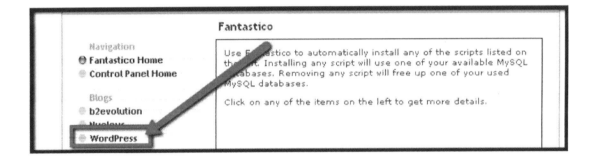

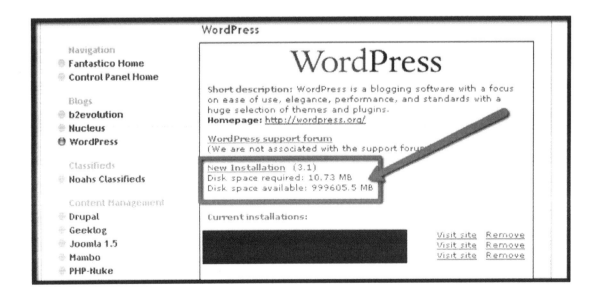

Use the drop-down menu to select the domain you want to install WordPress on. Leave the box for the directory blank unless you want to install WordPress on a subdomain as we discussed earlier. Leaving this blank is recommended in most cases.

Now enter your admin name (username) and password. Once again, the admin name you choose is permanent, but you will be able to change your display name later.

Moving on, choose your admin nickname (your display name) and your admin email. Your admin email will be the email address that you receive updates from WordPress on. You can use an existing email address or create one that exists on your domain, such as "admin@hockeyfans.com" for example.

Keep in mind that this email will get notifications on things such as users posting comments on your site, so it can be flooded fairly quickly in some cases. For this reason I would recommend not using an existing email account and instead creating a new one.

Now choose your site name and description. This will be the title and tagline that appear in your website's default header. You can choose to change these later if you want.

Once you're finished click "Install WordPress" and you're good to go. You can access your site by typing your domain name into the URL bar, and you can access your control panel login page by adding "/wp-admin" to the end of it, such as "www.hockeyfans.com/wp-admin."

As you can tell, installing WordPress on HostGator is just as quick and easy as it is on Bluehost.

Day 2 Recap

Here is what we went over today.

- What web hosting and servers are, and how they work
- That there are different web hosting companies to choose from
- Detailed information about Bluehost
- Detailed information about HostGator
- There are promo codes and discounts available for hosting; search for them on Google before signing up
- The difference between add-on domains and root domains
- What nameservers are and how to locate them
- How to go into your registrar account and set your nameservers
- It can take up to 72 hours before your domain shows up in your hosting cPanel after setting nameservers
- How to install WordPress on Bluehost and HostGator
- Your username is permanent, but you can change your display name
- How to access your WordPress control panel by adding "/wp-admin" to the end of your URL

Good job on getting your hosting set up and pointing your nameservers to it. Day 2 was a bit more technical than the previous day but overall still pretty simple. Always remember, if you are ever having any trouble with your web hosting account, contact customer service. Most companies have 24/7 support and can get back to you very quickly.

Day 3 – Setting Up WordPress

Today will be your first day actually logging in to WordPress and getting to know how to use it. I'll teach you the basic functions of the WordPress control panel and let you know which features are the most important. We'll also be going over how to create categories and sidebar links, how to use widgets, how to acquire and upload custom themes, and more.

As you can tell, we're going to be covering **a lot** of stuff today. The good news is that most of this is easy to understand, and I'll walk you through the more challenging parts like using FTP to upload files to your hosting server.

Chapter 6: Logging In and Updating WordPress

Logging in to WordPress is very simple once you have it installed on your domain name. The first thing you do is type in your URL followed by "/wp-admin" and you will get your login page, where you enter your username and password.

When you do this you have the option of checking the little box that says "remember me" so that when you come back to this page in the future you will already be logged in. This is obviously only advised on computers that are only used by you. Checking this box on shared computers or computers at a library or other public place presents a huge security risk.

If by chance you lose your password you can click the link that says "Lost your password?" and you will be given the opportunity to enter your username or email. You will then be sent an email allowing you to create a new password.

If by chance you forget your username *and* email you'll have to contact support to help you out. You can view the support page for this by clicking here. http://en.support.wordpress.com/contact/

You'll have to click on the buttons that say "I didn't find the right answer" a couple of times before the support form comes up.

Once you get logged in the very first thing you're going to want to do is update WordPress. There will most likely be a yellow bar across the top of the control panel prompting you to do this. Click "Please update now" and then click "Update Automatically" on the next page. WordPress will then update to the latest version.

WordPress 3.4.1 is available! Please update now.

Dashboard

There may also be some plugin and theme updates for you to do as well. Once again these are very simple, and a few clicks of the mouse will have you good to go. Whenever there is an update it appears on the left side of the black upper toolbar.

When you're logged in you can navigate away from the control panel and even close the browser, then come back to the control panel without having to log back in if you have cookies enabled in your browser. If you click away the tab or browser window for the control panel and don't return for an extended period of time, you will have to log back in, though.

You can log out at any time by mousing over the tab in the upper right hand corner that says "Howdy, [your username]" and then clicking on "Log Out" on the drop-down menu.

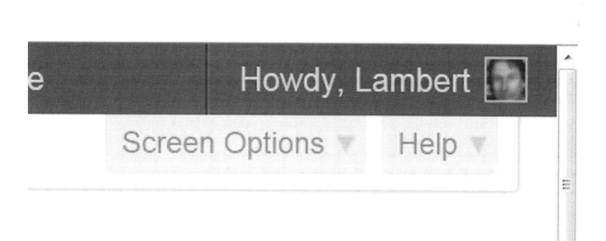

Chapter 7: Control Panel Basics

Now we're going to go over the basic function of most of the WordPress control panel. If something isn't mentioned here it is most likely because it will be discussed in greater detail later. Also, as we go through this chapter I'll be denoting which parts you should pay extra special attention to by writing (Very Important) next to them. These are the sections that you will really need to understand in order to build your website.

Edit Profile

The first thing you're going to want to do when you first log in to your control panel is to edit your profile. You can access your profile by mousing over the tab that says "Howdy, [your username]" that was just mentioned and then clicking "Edit My Profile."

Here you will have the option to change your admin color, enable keyboard shortcuts, enable/disable the toolbar (the black bar across the top) when viewing your actual site, and edit your contact information. Your profile also allows you to fill out your biographical information if you want to, as well as change your password.

Another important thing you can do here is to change your display name. You do this by entering what you want your display name to be in the field under "Name" that says "nickname." Then go down to the box that says "Display name publicly as" and select from between your username and nickname.

Once you are done with your profile click "Update Profile" at the bottom.

 Profile

Personal Options

Visual Editor   ☐ Disable the visual editor when writing

Admin Color Scheme   ○   Blue

                                ●   Gray

Keyboard Shortcuts   ☐ Enable keyboard shortcuts for comment moderation. More information

Toolbar   ☑ Show Toolbar when viewing site

Name

Username   lklein   *Usernames canno*

First Name   Lambert

Last Name   Klein

Nickname *(required)* ————————➤ lklein

Display name publicly as ————————➤ Lambert   ▾

Other Toolbar Options

Two more things that are located in the upper right hand corner of the black toolbar up top are the Screen Options and Help tabs. Screen Options allows you to alter the display of your control panel, including how many columns are on the page. Help is, as its name implies, what you click if you don't understand something.

Under the Help tab are two options that appear when you click on it, Documentation on Dashboard, which basically explains everything in the control panel like I'm doing, and Support Forums where you can sign up and discuss things with fellow WordPress users.

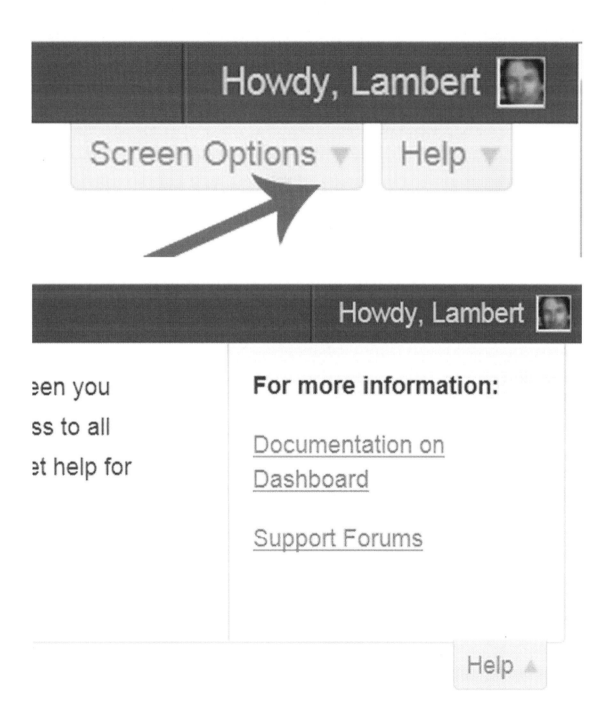

On the left-hand side of the black toolbar are several more options. The first is a WordPress logo that gives you the following options when moused over:

- About WordPress – info on the latest version of WordPress
- WordPress.org – a link to the main WordPress.org website
- Documentation – a link to information on how to use WordPress (very handy if you are a beginner)
- Support Forums – already explained
- Feedback – a link to the feedback section of the WordPress forums

Next to the WordPress logo you'll see the name of your website. Clicking this, or the drop-down tab that says Visit Site, will simply take you to the main page of your site. The little speech bubble notifies you of comments awaiting moderation while +New tab is just a shortcut to create a new Post, Link, Page, User, or add something to the Media Library.

As of right now most of these options aren't going to be needed though the Support Forums, and Documentation may come in handy in the future if you're trying to do something beyond the scope of this guide.

Also remember that if you need to update your plugins, or if you need to update your current version of WordPress, those notifications will appear in the black toolbar as well.

Your Dashboard

The Dashboard is the main page of your control panel and can be accessed at any time by clicking "Dashboard" in the upper left section of the main menu bar. Beneath the Dashboard tab are two options, Home, which takes you to the Dashboard same as clicking Dashboard itself, and Updates, which allows you to update WordPress when needed.

One thing to keep in mind about the menu bar on the left is that suboptions for each tab can be viewed by mousing over each tab. However, once a tab is selected its suboptions will display below it.

On your Dashboard you will see a variety of information regarding your website under the "Right Now" section on the left. Info that displays includes details on how many posts, pages, categories, and tags under Content as well as information on user comments under Discussion.

To the right of that is the QuickPress section, which allows you to quickly add a post instead of having to go through the Post process by using the Post tab on the left. This can be handy but lacks many of the features that you get when using the actual Post tab.

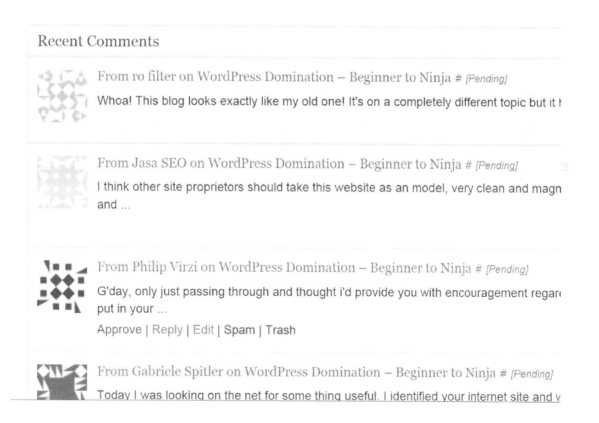

🏠 Dashboard

Screen Options ▼ Help ▼

Right Now ▼

Content

3 Posts
1 Page
1 Category
15 Tags

Discussion

98 Comments
0 Approved
81 Pending
17 Spam

Theme Flexibility3 with 7 Widgets

You are using **WordPress 3.4.1**

QuickPress

Title

Upload/Insert 📷

Content

Tags

Save Draft   Reset   **Publish**

Below Right Now are three more sections, Recent Comments, which shows recent comments, Incoming Links, which shows other blogs that have linked to your website, and Plugins, which gives a quick overview of what is going on in the world of WordPress plugins.

Recent Comments

From ro filter on WordPress Domination – Beginner to Ninja # *[Pending]*

Whoa! This blog looks exactly like my old one! It's on a completely different topic but it h

From Jasa SEO on WordPress Domination – Beginner to Ninja # *[Pending]*

I think other site proprietors should take this website as an model, very clean and magn and ...

From Philip Virzi on WordPress Domination – Beginner to Ninja # *[Pending]*

G'day, only just passing through and thought i'd provide you with encouragement regar put in your ...

Approve | Reply | Edit | Spam | Trash

From Gabriele Spitler on WordPress Domination – Beginner to Ninja # *[Pending]*

Today I was looking on the net for some thing useful. I identified your internet site and v

Do not rely on Incoming Links for analytics data once you start doing off-page SEO and building backlinks. There are more accurate programs and plugins available for that.

On the right-hand side of the Dashboard under QuickPress are several sections. Recent Drafts lists recent drafts of posts that you have created but have not actually published, WordPress Blog shows info from the official WordPress blog, and Other WordPress News is self-explanatory.

Recent Drafts

There are no drafts at the moment

WordPress Blog

Event Organizers Unite! July 13, 2012

I'm happy to announce the formation of a new official contributor group withii organizers of in-person events that promote WordPress. Though there are h organizing WordCamps, WordPress meetups, hackathons, free classes and all happening locally there was nev […]

WordPress 3.4.1 Maintenance and Security Release June 27, 2012

WordPress 3.4.1 is now available for download. WordPress 3.4 has been a ' flying off the shelf — 3 million downloads in two weeks! This maintenance re

Overall the Dashboard has some handy info on it, but truthfully you won't be spending a lot of time going over it. As previously mentioned there are more accurate analytics programs out there for gathering data on your website, and QuickPress is pretty useless in most cases unless you're just blogging for the fun of it. Although the Dashboard is the main page of your control panel, you won't be spending most of your time here.

Posts (Very Important!)

Clicking or mousing over the Posts tab under Dashboard on the menu to the left grants you access to several options. This is going to be one of your most-used sections in your WordPress control panel, because this is where you will upload and publish much of your new content to your website.

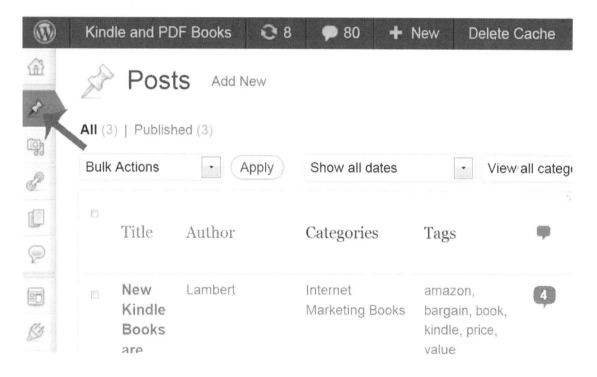

Clicking on "Posts" takes you to the posts page, which lists all of your published posts and drafts. These are posts that have been written but not published. Mousing over the title of each of your posts grants you several options: Edit, Quick Edit, Trash, and View. Edit takes you to the main editing/post creation page, Trash moves the post to the trash, and View allows you to view the post on your actual website.

Clicking on a post title takes you to the edit screen, which will be explained later when we discuss creating posts.

Quick Edit gives you fast access to several editing options such as Title, Date, Category, Tags, and more. This makes Quick Edit useless for editing the actual content but very efficient for editing specific data about the post itself. Click "Update" when you're done with a quick edit or "Cancel" to remove the Quick Edit screen.

You will also find other options on the Post page such as Bulk Actions, which allow you to Edit or Trash multiple posts at once. Keep in mind that when doing a Bulk Edit your options are very limited.

You can also filter your posts by their post dates and categories if you want. This can make it easier to find certain posts you're looking for sometimes.

The Search Posts option in the upper right hand corner allows you to quickly search for posts. Keep in mind that this option only searches the post titles, not the body.

Below the search box are two more options that allow you to configure how you view the posts page: list view (default) and excerpt view, which shows a brief excerpt of your post under each title.

Next to each individual post there will be information displayed showing the author, category, tags, number of comments, and the date. You can click on the author name to view all posts by that author, the category to view all posts in that category, and the tags to view all posts that share a certain tag. Clicking on comments will take you to a page allowing you to view the comments for that post.

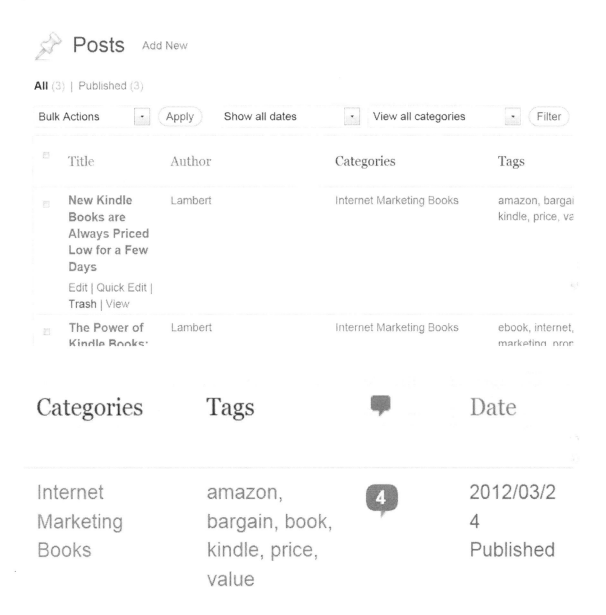

Underneath the All Posts tab is the Add New tab. Clicking this will take you to the post creation/editing page. We'll get into that a bit later.

Below Add New is the Categories tab. This tab opens up a page allowing you to edit and create categories. Categories are important on WordPress because they allow your visitor to easily navigate your website and access similar posts and pages that are related to one another.

Overall you probably won't be using the Category tab very often. Categories are more easily created when you create posts. If you do need to manage your categories, this is the place to do it.

Adding a new category consists of creating its name and choosing a "slug," which is basically a URL-friendly name if you need one. In most cases the slug will simply be the category name in lowercase letters with hyphens between each word. You can also make a new category the child category of an existing category by selecting the "Parent" drop-down menu. In most cases this is unnecessary.

Beneath that is a field where you can write a description for your category. This is mostly unnecessary as well, and most themes will not show the description by default, although some will.

To the right is an area where you can use Bulk Actions to delete multiple categories if you need to. There is also a search box allowing you to search for categories by name.

Show on screen

☑ Description ☑ Slug ☑ Posts

20   Categories   (Apply)

Screen Options ▴

🖈 Categories

(Search Categories)

Bulk Actions | · | (Apply)   *1 item*

☐	Name	Description	Slug	Posts
	Internet Marketing Books		internetbooks	3

In addition, you can mouse over each category for more options: Edit, Quick Edit, Delete, and View. Edit allows you to edit your category on a screen similar to the one used to create categories. Quick Edit allows you to quickly edit a category's name and slug, while View takes you to a page on your website where all posts in a specific category are shown. You can also click on the number under Posts to view all posts in a category. Delete will of course delete the category

The Tags tab is very similar to the Categories tab in many ways. When you click on it a page opens that allows you to create new tags and edit existing tags. You won't be using this much since you will, more often than not, be creating tags as you create posts.

Tags are basically terms you apply to your posts that you want search engines to associate them with. We'll talk about this a bit later when we get into SEO. For now just know that you can create and edit tags here.

Media

Under the Posts tab is the Media tab. This section allows you to upload media files such as images, audio files, video files, and more. In most cases you will be adding these files as you create your posts and pages, but if you ever need to upload a bunch of files all at once, this is where you do it.

The main page of the Media tab shows all the items in your media library and allows you to edit them. Mousing over each file presents you with the options: Edit, Delete Permanently, and View. Delete Permanently and View are self-explanatory, while Edit opens a new page and allows you to change basic info such as the name, description, and URL of the file. You can also access some advanced editing features by clicking on the Edit button on the new page that opens up.

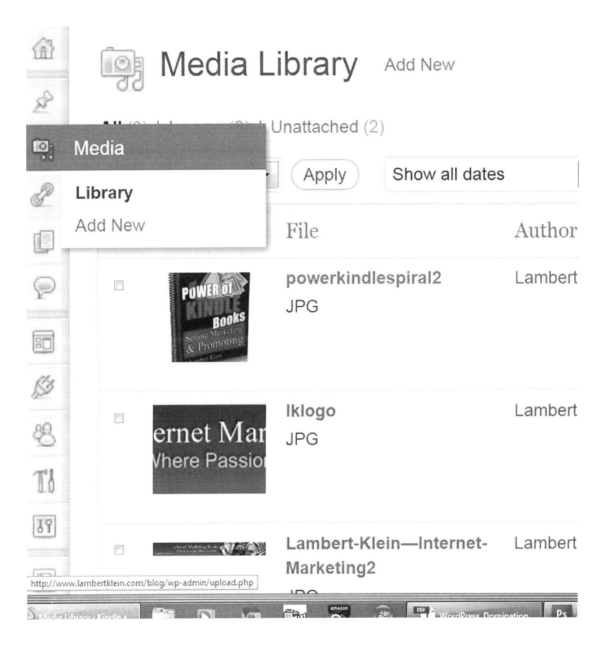

You can also do bulk deletes on the Main page, filter the page by date, and use the search box to find specific files.

You can click on the posts that each media file is attached to, as well as view pending comments on each file.

Below the "Library" tab in the menu to the left you'll find the Add New tab. This opens a new page that allows you to add new media files using the "Select Files" button or by dragging and dropping them into the field. In most cases you will be adding files per post instead of here.

Links

This tab, which appears beneath Media, allows you to manage some of the links on your site. For the most part this section is irrelevant, as there are better ways to add links if you need to. The only major exception would occur if you decide to charge people to link your site to theirs in the future, in which case the Links tab can be a handy way to create and manage these links.

Pages (Very Important)

The Pages tab under Links allows you to create and manage your website's pages. Pages are different from posts, and we'll get into that a bit later, but for now just think of "pages" as pages on your website like "About," "Privacy Policy," "Contact," and stuff like that. Clicking the Pages tab opens a page that allows you to create and manage pages like these.

Pages	Add New				

All (1) | Published (1)

Bulk Actions ▾	Apply	Show all dates ▾	Filter

	Author	💬	Date	SEO Title
Pages				
All Pages	Lambert	5	2012/01/04 Published	
Add New				

☐	Title	Author	💬	Date	SEO Title

Bulk Actions ▾	Apply

To view and edit your page select the All Pages tab. This opens a page that looks very similar to the All Posts tab, and they function virtually the same. Mousing over a page gives you the same options: Edit, Quick Edit, Trash, and View. The bulk actions, filter, and search bar are all the same as well.

Clicking on a page title or the "Edit" option takes you to the page editor/creator, which is also pretty much identical to the post editor/creator. Clicking Add New under the All Pages tab also takes you here.

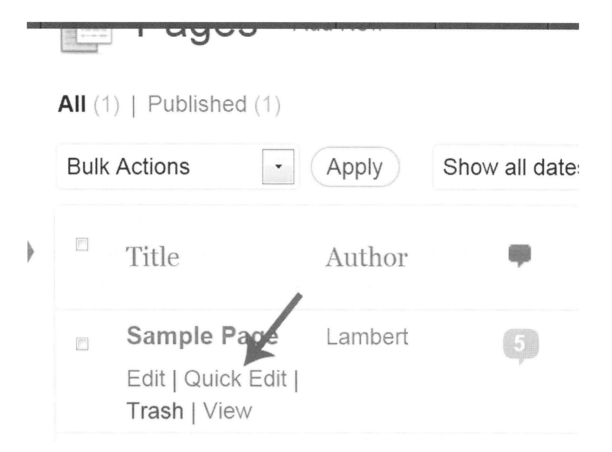

One important thing to remember about pages is that, unlike posts, when you create a page it typically shows up in the navigation bar on your website. This can be disabled by editing the CSS in order to create hidden pages, but it's easier to just use the Exclude Pages plugin.

http://wordpress.org/extend/plugins/exclude-pages/

Also keep in mind that there can be parent and child pages in addition to standalone pages. This is great for situations in which you need certain pages to belong to a certain category or section of your website.

Comments

The comments section is where you can manage the comments you get on your website's posts if you allow them. This section is virtually identical to previous sections of the Dashboard, so we're not going to spend too much time on it. Comments awaiting approval will show up in this section.

An interesting thing you can do here is view the IP address of the person who made the post and their email address. Mousing over the comment gives you more options: Unapprove/Approve, Reply, Edit, Quick Edit, Spam, and Trash. Selecting "Spam" will save spam comments in your database to help spam blockers block spam more easily in the future.

You actually can go in and edit other people's comments. This isn't advised though, and if someone makes a comment you don't like you should simply delete it if you feel the need to do that.

Appearance (Very Important)

The Appearance tab is a very important tab, as it will allow you to access options to configure your theme. Clicking on the tab opens the Manage Themes page, which allows you to control which theme is currently active on your website. By default WordPress comes with two themes, Twenty Eleven 1.3 and Twenty Ten 1.3. These themes are decent, but you should get something better. We'll discuss getting custom themes a bit later.

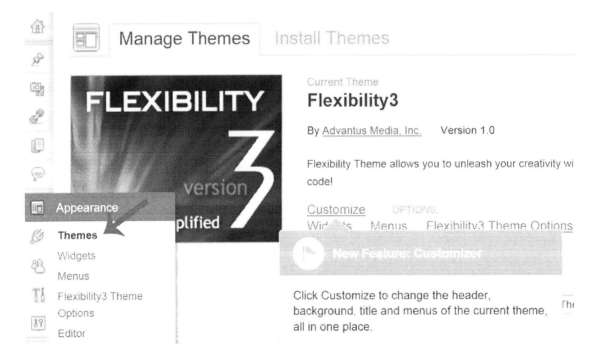

Any custom themes you install will appear on the Manage Themes page as well, with your active theme appearing at the top. The options available to you will depend on what theme you're using.

On this page you can also click on the Install Themes tab up top to access a new page in which you can install new themes, among other things. The default page is the Search page that allows you to search for new themes to use. I feel it's more efficient to use Google or another search engine to find new themes to use.

Next to "Search" is "Upload," which allows you to upload themes from your hard drive. You can also upload themes via a FTP program like Filezilla. We will go over this later.

The next option is "Featured," which will allow you to choose from some featured custom themes that WordPress is promoting. Next to this is "Newest," which features the newest themes available. Lastly there is "Recently Updated" which, as its name implies, shows recently updated themes.

Widgets (Very Important)

Under the Appearance tab to the left you will find Widgets, when you have Appearance selected or if you mouse over Appearance. Clicking on Widgets allows you to basically insert custom fields into your website, most of them in the sidebars.

There are many different Widgets, and since the Widgets page gives a description of each one I'm not going to go over what each one does here.

Widgets

Available Widgets

Drag widgets from here to a sidebar on the right to activate them. Drag widgets back here to deactivate them and delete their settings.

Archives

...e of your site's posts

Appearance

Themes

Widgets

Menus

Flexibility3 Theme Options

Editor

...r site's posts

...n of categories

http://www.lambertklein.com/blog/wp-admin/themes.php

Sidebar_top

Search

Sidebar_left

Sidebar_right

Feature_top

On the Widgets page you will also see a section to the right that has several fields such as Primary Widget Area, First Footer, and more. The options you have available in this section are determined by your theme, and using a custom theme can grant you a completely different set of options.

To add a Widget to your website, simply drag the one you want from the selection of widgets to the area that you want it to appear in. For example, if you want an RSS widget to appear in the top sidebar, click on RSS and drag it over to Secondary Widget Area.

Once you do this you will notice that new options become available. These options will be different depending on which widget you use. Most of these options are self-explanatory and easy to understand. Once you've chosen the options you want and have filled out the information, click "save" to save your widget, and it will appear on your website in the area you chose.

ate them and delete their settings.

Categories

A list or dropdown of categories

Meta

Log in/out, admin, feed and WordPress links

Recent Posts

The most recent posts on your site

Tag Cloud

Your most used tags in cloud format

Sidebar_top

Search

Sidebar_left

Sidebar_right

Recent Posts: Current Topics

Text: Kindle Books

Tag Cloud: Topics

Text: Contact

Sidebar_right ▾

Recent Posts: Current Topics ▾

Title:

Current Topics

Number of posts to show: 5

Delete | Close ➡ **Save**

The Text widget is special because not only does it allow you to enter text, it also allows you to enter HTML, which opens up a lot of opportunities for customization, such as adding social like buttons, opt-in forms, and more.

Text: Kindle Books

Title:

Kindle Books

```
Kindle Books</h3>
    <div class="aligncenter">
     <p><a href="http://www.amazon.com/dp/B007LS0TLE"
target="_blank"><img src="../images/wpdomination-redbar200.jpg"
width="200" height="266" alt="WordPress Beginner to
Ninja" /></a><br />
     Just Released!</p>
    </div>
    <p> 
  </p>
    <div class="wasocial_facebook_like">
     <div id="fb-root"></div>
     <script
src="http://connect.facebook.net/en_US/all.js#xfbml=1"></script>
```

☐ Automatically add paragraphs

Delete | Close   Save

To delete a widget simply click on it to open it up, then click delete. You can also simply drag the widget back out of the area, if you want.

Menus

Underneath the Widgets tab you will find Menus. This tab simply opens up a page that shows your Links, Pages, and Categories. It also allows you to create custom menus, if you'd like. Overall this section isn't that important unless you want to create a new menu.

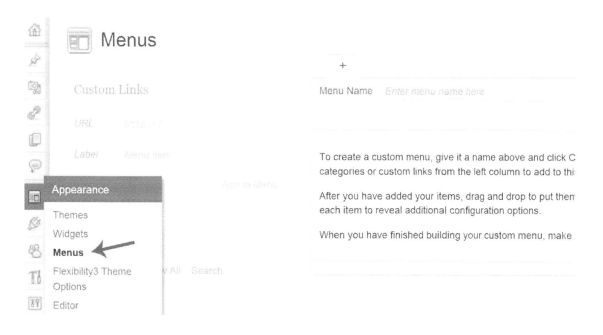

Also note that certain custom themes will have their own options available. In most cases these options will appear beneath the Menus tab, but in some cases they can appear elsewhere, it just depends on the theme you're using.

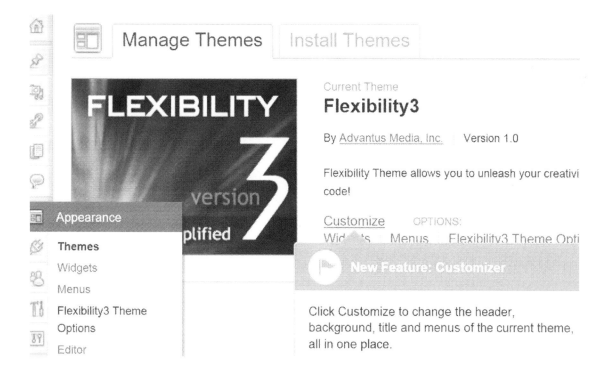

Next are the Header and Background links. Sometimes having a custom theme installed will cause these to disappear, and you'll have to install your header and background through the theme configuration settings.

Current Theme

Twenty Ten

By the WordPress team | Version 1.3

The 2010 theme for WordPress is stylish, customizable, si̇ — make it yours with a custom menu, header image, and b Twenty Ten supports six widgetized areas (two in the sideŀ footer) and featured images (thumbnails for gallery posts a images for posts and pages). It includes stylesheets for pri̇ Visual Editor, special styles for posts in the "Asides" and "C and has an optional one-column page template that remov

There is a new version of Twenty Ten available. View v or **update now.**

Customize   OPTIONS:
Widgets | Menus | Header | Background

The final tab underneath Appearance is the Editor tab. This allows you to actively edit the CSS of your theme to change the appearance. If you don't understand CSS, you should leave this alone as you could mangle your theme pretty badly if you get in there and start messing around with stuff.

There are certain things that can be done here even if you don't understand CSS, such as configuring your website to show excerpts of posts on your main page instead of complete posts. Little tricks like this are handy to know, and in some cases you will be expected to edit CSS in order to get certain plugins to work with certain themes.

Also don't forget that you can edit any theme you have installed on WordPress, not just your active theme, by using the theme selector to the right.

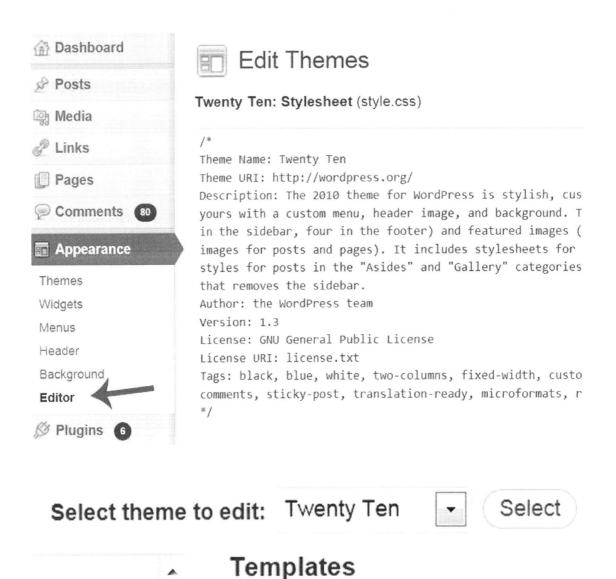

Plugins (Very Important)

The next tab in the menu to the left is Plugins, and this is where you can manage, search, and install plugins for your site. Plugins are basically programs that perform specific functions on your site, such as catching spam, making navigation easier, and much more.

Also notice that if you need to update a plugin, a little black circle will appear next to the Plugins tab with a number in it. The number is the number of plugins that require your attention.

By default you start with two plugins: Hello Dolly and Akismet. Hello Dolly simply displays random lyrics from the famous song sung by Louis Armstrong, while Akismet filters spam. Hello Dolly can be deleted because it is functionally useless. Akismet now requires you to go through some stuff such as registering and receiving an activation code to use, so keep that in mind. There are other spam filter plugins available, should you decide to delete Akismet.

To delete a plugin you must first deactivate it. You can do this by clicking the deactivate option underneath it. You can also edit the code of most plugins, but this is not advised unless you have a very thorough understanding of this sort of thing. Otherwise you will probably just end up making your plugin nonfunctional.

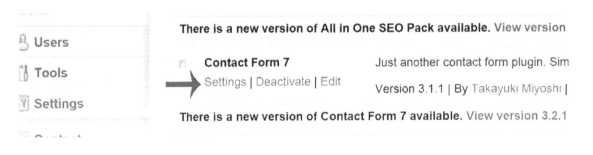

Keep in mind that some plugins will have a "Settings" option that allows you to configure them. In some cases this will appear down next to the Delete and Edit options, but in other cases it will appear in a completely different section of the WordPress control panel. It just depends on the plugin. Many plugins' options show up in the Settings tab in the main menu on the control panel.

To find new plugins you can either search for them in Google or another search engine, then upload them via FTP, or you can simply click Add New and do a search for the plugin you're looking for and install it through your control panel.

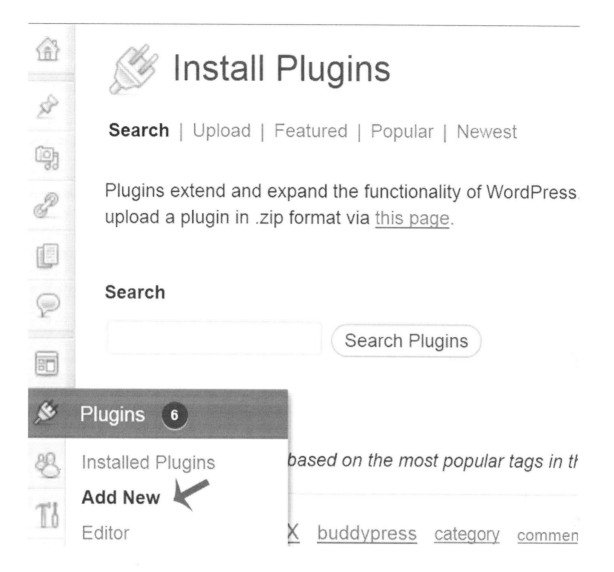

Install Plugins

Search | Upload | Featured | Popular | Newest

Plugins extend and expand the functionality of WordPress. upload a plugin in .zip format via this page.

Search

[   ]   (Search Plugins)

Plugins ⑥

Installed Plugins   *based on the most popular tags in th*

Add New

Editor   X buddypress category commen

While installing via your control panel is the easier way to do things, occasionally it can be hard to find the plugin you want using the search option.

When you do a search, a new page will come up listing several plugins that match your criteria. You'll be able to get more details on the plugin, install it right away, and check the rating the plugin has. Make sure you read the description to verify that a plugin is what you are looking for before installing. If you install a plugin that you don't want or need, simply deactivate it and delete it.

Users

The next tab is the Users tab. This allows you to manage your profile and add new users to your site. Adding a new user is handy in two ways. First, it allows you to create another profile for yourself that you can use to post under different usernames if you wish.

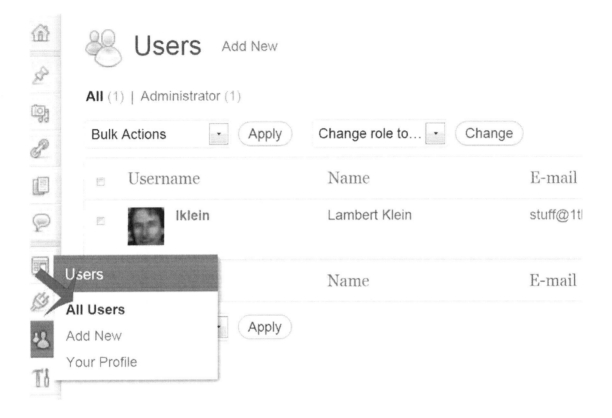

The second thing you can do is create special user accounts for others if you need to let someone else have access to the control panel but don't want them to have full administrative control over the site. Clicking "Add New" will take you to the page where you can create a new account, and at the bottom you will see a drop-down menu that allows you to determine what privileges the user will have. This is incredibly handy if you're outsourcing content creation or hiring someone to change the layout of your site.

Add New User

Create a brand new user and add it to this site.

Username *(required)*

E-mail *(required)*

First Name

Last Name

Website

Password *(twice, required)*

Tools

The Tools section is where you'll find tools that do various things for WordPress. By default you'll have Press This, which allows you to quickly and easily take content from the web and publish it on your site. This can be handy if you're creating a content curation site.

The other tool you get is Categories and Tags Converter. This simply allows you to convert tags to categories and vice versa.

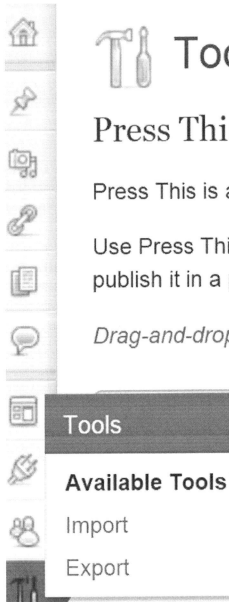

Tools

Press This

Press This is a bookmarklet: a little app that rur

Use Press This to clip text, images and videos 1
publish it in a post on your site.

Drag-and-drop the following link to your bookm

Tools

Available Tools

Import

Export

Tags Converter

your categories to tags (c

Below the main tab you'll find two more tabs, Import and Export. Import allows
you to import a variety of things onto your site, such as Blogger blog posts,
Tumblr posts, and more. This can be handy if you want this information to be
reposted on your WordPress site.

Import

If you have posts or comments in another system, WordPres
from below:

Blogger	Install the Blogger impo
Blogroll	Install the blogroll impor
Categories and Tags Converter	Install the category/tag (selectively.
LiveJournal	Install the LiveJournal ir
Movable Type and TypePad	Install the Movable Type blog.
Tools	Install the RSS importer
Available Tools	Install the Tumblr impor
Import ←	Install the WordPress in tags from a WordPress
Export	

Export allows you to export various bits of data such as pages, comments, and more as an XML file. Once you export your data you can then import it onto another WordPress site.

🔨 Export

When you click the button below WordPress

This format, which we call WordPress eXtenc
tags.

Once you've saved the download file, you ca

Choose what to export

⦿ All content

This will contain all of your posts, pages, con

○ Posts

○ Pages

○ Contact Forms

(Download Export File)

Also be aware that some of your plugins will have their settings and options
show up here in the Tools section. If you install a plugin and its options don't
show up in the Plugins section, check here and in the Settings tab below.

Settings (Very Important)

The final tab in the left menu is the Settings tab. This tab allows you to change many of the fundamental properties of your website. Most of this comes down to personal preference, although there are a few things you're going to want to do a certain way for SEO purposes and that will be explained a bit later.

The first sub-tab is General, which allows you to change things such as your site's title, date, and time, email address, and much more. Everything here is pretty self-explanatory, but just make sure your time zone is set correctly, as this can impact how certain plugins work if they require a cron job.

General Settings

Site Title	Kindle and PDF Books
Tagline	Internet Marketing Books
	In a few words, explain what this site is abc
WordPress Address (URL)	http://www.lambertklein.com/blog
Site Address (URL)	http://www.lambertklein.com/blog
	Enter the address here if you want your site
	installed WordPress.
E-mail Address	stuff@1thinkhealthy.com
	This address is used for admin purposes, li
Membership	☐ Anyone can register

The next subtab is Writing, which allows you to configure some options that affect the creation of your posts. Everything here is also explained on the page.

Writing Settings

Size of the post box	40 lines
Formatting	☑ Convert emoticons like :-) and :-P to graphics on display
	☐ WordPress should correct invalidly nested XHTML automatically
Default Post Category	Internet Marketing Books ▾
Default Post Format	Standard ▾
Default Link Category	Interesting Places ▾

Press This

Press This is a bookmarklet: a little app that runs in your browser and lets you grab bits of the web.

Use Press This to clip text, images and videos from any web page. Then edit and add more straight from Press

The next sub-tab is the Reading tab. This section is going to be very important when it comes to configuring how your website's posts display. The first option allows you to choose to display either your blog posts or a static page as your home page. This really comes down to personal preference, and we'll go into this in more detail later.

You can also configure how many blog posts your "posts page" (by default your main page) displays. This is great for editing your site to ensure that you don't have a ridiculous number of posts displayed on your main page.

Reading Settings

Front page displays	• Your latest posts
	◦ A static page (select below)
	Front page: — Select — ▾
	Posts page: — Select — ▾
Blog pages show at most	10 posts
Syndication feeds show the most recent	10 items
For each article in a feed, show	• Full text
	◦ Summary

The next sub-tab is the Discussions tab. This page allows you to configure various things having to do with the comments on your site. There is nothing particularly important here.

Next is the Media subtab. This section allows you to configure a few things that have to do with your media files, such as image thumbnail size and other things. Once again, this is simply a matter of personal preference.

The next sub-tab is Privacy. This allows you to set whether or not search engines can index your site. **Make sure that this is turned on**! If the search engines can't index your site then you won't appear in the search results and won't get organic traffic.

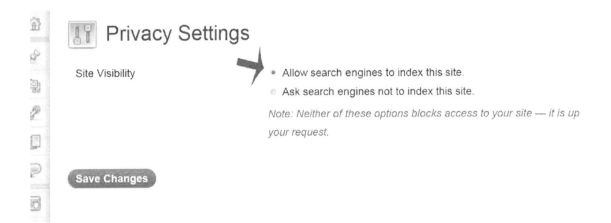

The Permalinks sub-tab allows you to configure how your URL extensions display. For example, a page can display as

www.hockeyfans.com/throwback-jerseys

www.hockeyfans.com/2012/03/throwback-jerseys

www.hockeyfans.com/p=1

The way you set this up is **very** important for SEO. There is an entire chapter coming up dedicated to making sure you set up your permalinks correctly and why you're going to do it that way.

After permalinks you will usually see any settings for plugins you have that appear in this section. Under that you'll find a little button that says "Collapse menu" that will simply move the left-hand menu to the side and out of the way if you need that.

Chapter 8: Setting Permalinks

As promised, this is the chapter dedicated to setting your permalinks and explaining why it is so important. This is one of the most fundamental parts of on-site SEO, and botching this can cripple your efforts to rank in Google and other search engines. The good news is that this is very easy to implement.

By default your permalinks are set to "?p=123" and this setting will cause your entire page and post URLs to be displayed as the extension "/p=1" or whatever page number it happens to be. This is terrible for SEO because "/p=1" tells the search engine spiders that crawl your site absolutely nothing about your page or post.

You want your URL extensions to give an indicator of what your post or page is about so that it can rank for those keywords in Google and other search engines. For example, the URL "www.hockeyfans.com/throwback-jerseys" tells the search engine spiders that the page/post is about throwback jerseys. This will help the site to rank for that term.

To set up your site to display URLs like this, go to the Permalinks subtab under Settings and go down to where it says Custom Structure. Click that bubble and enter this:

%postname%

Doing this will cause the name of your post or page to show up as the URL extension, not "/p=2" or something like that.

This also makes choosing your post titles wisely very important. Because you want your keywords in your URLs, you have to also make sure they're in your post titles. Because this is such a fundamental part of successful WordPress SEO, I encourage you to do this right now so that you don't forget.

Chapter 9: Creating Categories and Sidebar Links

You should familiarize yourself with how to create categories and sidebar links. These features will show up in your sidebars using widgets and are pretty easy to configure.

Categories

Categories are basically just a way of organizing your posts and making navigation a bit easier for your views. For example, you may have a category on www.hockeyfans.com called "Highlights" that contains all posts related to game highlights. You could also have a category called "Red Wings" if you want to group all posts about the Red Wings.

Keep in mind that a post can fall into more than one category. For example, if you're making a post about the highlights of a Red Wings game, you can place that into both of the previously mentioned categories.

To create categories you can click the Posts tab, then click the Categories sub-tab. Here you can create the title, slug, and description of new categories as well as edit existing categories like we talked about earlier.

Keep in mind that you don't have to create all of your categories all at once here, and you can create them on the go as you make new posts. To do this, click on Add New under the Posts tab to begin creating a new post. Scroll down and you will see the Categories box on the right. Here you get to select what category your post falls into as well as create a new category if you want. You can also view your most-used categories by clicking the Most Used tab.

Categories

Add New Category

Name

The name is how it appears on your site.

Slug

The "slug" is the URL-friendly version of the name. It is usually all lowercase and contains only letters, numbers, and hyphens.

Bulk Actions · Apply

☐ Name Desc

Internet Marketing Books

☐ Name Desc

Bulk Actions · Apply

Note:

Deleting a category does not delete th...

Sidebars

You are also going to want to ensure that your categories show up in your sidebar links. You do this by creating a categories widget in the Widgets section. Other links that you will definitely want to have in your sidebar are your archives, which allow viewers to access older posts.

You can also link viewers to other things in the sidebar such as recent posts, recent comments, other web accounts you have such as Facebook, and other people's blogs/websites if they're paying you to advertise for them.

Because creating these sidebar links is done using widgets, we'll discuss that next.

Chapter 10: Using Widgets

We've already gone over a lot about widgets, but I'm going to walk you through the creation of a few of them just to help you get the hang of it. The first widget you're going to create is the Categories widget, which will list links to all your categories.

The first step is simple. Go to Appearance, then click on Widgets. Once you're in the widgets section you need to think about which section you're going to place your Categories widget in. The most common choice would be Primary Widget Area, but because it is likely that there is a Categories widget in there by default, let's put it in another area. If you have a custom theme already installed there may be other options too. In the end this is a matter of personal preference.

Once you've made up your mind, go get the Categories widget and drag it over to the section you want it to appear in. This will bring up some new options.

Widgets

Available Widgets	Primary Widget Area
Drag widgets from here to a sidebar on the right to activate them. Drag widgets back here to deactivate them and delete their settings.	The primary widget area
Archives A monthly archive of your site's posts	**Search**
Calendar A calendar of your site's posts	Secondary Widget Area
Categories A list or dropdown of categories	First Footer Widget Area
Custom Menu	Second Footer Widget Area

Screen Option

The title will be the title of the widget, and I'd recommend just using "Categories." The "Display as drop-down" option will make the widget display as a drop-down menu that must be selected in order to see the categories. This is only good if you are really cramped for space on your website. "Show post counts" will show the number of posts in each category and "Show hierarchy" will cause the categories to display with the child categories underneath the parent categories, if you have created parent and child categories.

Once you're done click "Save." Now click on your website's title in the upper-left corner on the black toolbar to make sure the widget is displaying the way you want it to. If it isn't, go back and try again. Sometimes you have to play around with it for a while before you get it displaying the way you want it to.

The next widget we're going to create is the Tag Cloud widget. Tag Cloud is a widget that displays all of your tags in the sidebar. This is good for SEO because these tags will show up on every single page and post of your website to help the spiders rank your pages for more keywords.

Once you have an idea of which sidebar section you want your tag cloud to go in, drag the Tag Cloud widget over to it. Once again, new options will appear.

Archives

A monthly archive of your site's posts

Calendar

A calendar of your site's posts

Categories

A list or dropdown of categories

Custom Menu

Use this widget to add one of your custom menus as a widget.

Links

Your blogroll

Search

Secondary Widget Area

The secondary widget area

Tag Cloud

Title:

Taxonomy:

Tags

Delete | Close   Save

You can create the title of your tag cloud here as well as change it from displaying tags to displaying categories. This isn't recommended, as your categories should have their own widget. Once you're done click "Save" and then check your site to see if the widget is displaying how you want it to.

Overall using widgets is very easy but can take some getting used to in order to make sure they're displaying where you want them to. Also, configuring how your widgets look on your site can be a bit like fitting together the pieces of a puzzle sometimes. Just play around with widget creation a while, and you'll soon get the hang of it.

Widgets

Screen Option

Available Widgets

Drag widgets from here to a sidebar on the right to activate them. Drag widgets back here to deactivate them and delete their settings.

Archives

A monthly archive of your site's posts

Calendar

A calendar of your site's posts

Categories

A list or dropdown of categories

Custom Menu

Primary Widget Area

The primary widget area

Search

Secondary Widget Area

First Footer Widget Area

Second Footer Widget Area

Chapter 11: Setting Up Themes

When you first install WordPress your default theme is going to be Twenty Ten. Twenty Eleven will also be installed (after updating to the latest version of WordPress) and can be activated from the Themes tab. These themes are decent, but there are better themes available. In some cases you're going to want to get a particular theme that is based around your business model, such as an AdSense theme for Google AdSense.

Getting a Theme

As we briefly touched on earlier, there are several ways to go about getting new themes. You can browse themes from your WordPress control panel by clicking the Install tab on the Themes page. You can then browse a variety of themes by clicking on the options there.

The other way of getting themes is to look for them on Google or another search engine. Using a search term such as "WordPress themes" or "free WordPress themes" is a great way to search. Also keep in mind that not all themes are free, but just because a theme must be purchased doesn't necessarily make it superior to a free theme.

These themes will have to be downloaded to your hard drive, then uploaded to WordPress using a FTP client. We'll discuss that in the next chapter.

When choosing a theme try to pick something that fits your website. Also, remember that you can go back and change your theme later if you feel like it. If you're having trouble picking a theme for your site, try browsing around and checking out what similar sites are using.

Two popular themes that work well for a variety of websites are Thesis http://diythemes.com/ and Flexibility http://www.flexibilitytheme.com/ . Click the links to check them out. They're great all-around themes that can be used with a variety of monetization methods. This makes them a good choice to start with if you haven't yet decided how you're going to monetize your site. I recommend getting at least one of them (Flexibility is free), because I'll be walking you through how to use FTP to upload a theme in the next chapter.

Activating and Editing Themes

Once you upload a theme it can be activated from the Themes page by selecting the Manage Themes tab. Then click on the "Activate" option.

By the WordPress team   Version 1.3

The 2010 theme for WordPress is stylish, customizable, s
menu, header image, and background. Twenty Ten suppc
footer) and featured images (thumbnails for gallery posts a
includes stylesheets for print and the admin Visual Editor,
categories, and has an optional one-column page templat

There is a new version of Twenty Ten available. View

Customize   OPTIONS Widgets   Menus   He

Available Themes

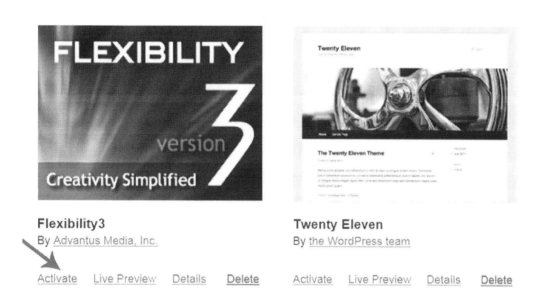

Flexibility3
By Advantus Media, Inc.

Activate   Live Preview   Details   Delete

Twenty Eleven
By the WordPress team

Activate   Live Preview   Details   Delete

Your active theme will appear up above the other installed themes. Depending
on what theme you have installed, you may get some extra configuration
options.

New theme activated. This theme supports widgets, please visit the widgets settings screen to configure them.

Current Theme
Flexibility3

By Advantus Media, Inc.   Version 1.0

Flexibility Theme allows you to unleash your creativity without having to know code!

Customize   OPTIONS Widgets   Menus   Flexibility3 Theme Options

Most themes allow you to install a custom header, which you should do as soon as possible to make your site look more professional. Most themes will also allow you to upload a background if you'd like to. Additionally you can go into the actual CSS and configure a theme from there, as we discussed earlier. Once again, don't do this if you don't understand CSS.

Because different themes have different options and settings, this is something you will have to play around with and figure out on your own. Generally speaking, there are several guidelines to follow when configuring your theme.

- Keep the layout clean and simple
- Don't add pointless widgets and images
- Don't add a distracting background
- Add a professional-looking header
- Choose an attractive color scheme (colorschemedesigner.com can help)

Choosing and configuring a WordPress theme takes more than just technical knowhow, it also takes an understanding of basic graphic design. If you're having trouble and just can't get your theme and layout to look right, don't forget that you can outsource this. Most web designers don't charge a lot just to quickly configure a theme for you. Header design and your background graphic can also be outsourced easily using Fiverr.com.

Chapter 12: File Uploading Using FTP and cPanel

While themes and plugins can be uploaded directly from the WordPress control panel, there may come a time when you have to upload the file from your hard drive and directly into your hosting account. There are generally two ways to do this: FTP (file transfer protocol) and using the cPanel itself.

The Difference Between Root Domains and Add-on Domains

While there is very little fundamental difference between a root domain and an add-on domain, the file path you use to access each of these is different. Just to be clear, the very first domain that you install your web hosting server on is the root domain. Any domains you install after that are add-on domains.

cPanel

Using the cPanel will be different for each hosting company, so I'm not really going to get into that. In most cases though you will have to access your domains via your cPanel and then get into the Public HTML folder. If you're really struggling to upload files through your cPanel, try looking up tutorials online, particularly on YouTube. Alternately you can just do it using FTP, which is much easier.

While getting into your files via cPanel is going to be different depending on what host you have, you typically want to try to find a file manager and open that up. Here are the different file paths for your root domain and add-on domains.

Root Domain:

root/ → public_html → wp_content → themes

Add-on Domain:

root/ → public_html → [name of add-on domain] → wp_content → themes

Remember, this is just an example, and different hosting services may have different file paths. If you're having trouble figuring out the file path for your web hosting, contact customer support and they'll help you out.

FTP

File transfer protocol (FTP) allows you to quickly and easily upload files to your website using an FTP program. I recommend Filezilla, which you can download for free by clicking here.
http://filezilla-project.org/

Filezilla is easy to use, but I'll walk you through how to upload a theme to your WordPress site. The first thing you need to do once you get Filezilla installed on your computer is to connect to your web hosting server. You do this by entering the following information:

- Host – Your server's IP address or your root domain name
- Username – Your username used to log in to your cPanel
- Password – Your password used to log in to your cPanel
- Port – You only need to enter this if it is *not* the default port. In most cases you can just leave this blank.

If you don't know your hosting server's IP address, it can usually be found on the main page of your cPanel. If you can't find it there, check the first email that your web host sent you that had your nameservers in it. Your IP address should be in there as well in most cases.

An alternate method of entering the "Host" info is to enter the root domain on which the server is connected to. For example, if when you first signed up you connected your web hosting to the domain cats.com then you can enter cats.com in the host field.

Remember, this only works for the root domain that your hosting is connected to, not necessarily the domain your website is on. For example, if your root domain is cats.com but the domain you're building your WordPress site on is hockeyfans.com you can't use hockeyfans.com to access your hosting server via FTP, because it is an add-on domain, not the root domain.

Once all the info is entered click "Quick Connect" and Filezilla will hook up to your hosting server, giving you access to all the files found there. Now what you're going to do is get into the files for the domain you're building your WordPress site on. I'll go over how to do this for add-on domains first because it is slightly more complicated.

Below the connection data area you'll see four fields. The two on the left are files on your computer. The two on the right are files on your hosting server. The ones on top help you navigate, while the larger ones on the bottom are for transferring specific files. For this example we'll be transferring a theme from your computer to the hosting server.

The first thing you need to do is go into the files on the left and locate the WordPress theme you downloaded. Once you've found your theme the specific folder containing all the files should appear in the lower-left box. Make sure the file is unzipped if you downloaded a zipped file.

After you find your theme go to the upper-right area and click the folder found there that is labeled "/". This should open several subfolders in the lower-right area as well as in the upper area. Ignore the folders in the lower area for a moment and concentrate on the folders in the upper area. Scroll down and you should see a folder labeled "public_html." Double-click that.

Once you're in this folder you should see more folders. Find the one that is labeled with the domain name you're building your WordPress site on, and click that. More folders will appear, and find the one that says "wp-content" and click that. More folders will appear, and find the one that says "themes" and click that. Also take note of the folder that says "plugins" here, as you will need to use that folder to install plugins later.

Once you are in the themes folder you can upload your theme. Right click on your themes folder and select "Upload." This will upload your theme into the theme folder on your file hosting. That's all there is to it.

Just to recap, for add-on domains the file path to get to the themes folder in your hosting server is:

root/ → public_html → [the add-on domain name] → wp-content → themes.

The file path for root domains is:

root/ → public_html → wp_content → themes

Keep in mind that this might not be exactly the same for every hosting service. If your hosting is drastically different from the steps outlined here, try looking up some tutorials on YouTube, visiting the forums if there are any, or contacting customer support if you have to.

In addition to using the Quick Connect feature on Filezilla you can also configure specific connection profiles by clicking File then Site Manager. This is good if you will be sharing Filezilla or your computer with others and want to make sure that no one else has access to your web hosting files.

Day 3 Recap

Here is what we went over today.

- How to log in to WordPress using your domain name and "/wp-admin"
- All of the basic functions of the WordPress control panel
- The difference between posts and pages
- How to set your permalinks for good on-site SEO
- What categories are and how to create them
- How to use widgets
- How to acquire and set up your theme
- The difference between uploading files using FTP and your cPanel
- The difference between root domains and add-on domains
- How to upload files using Filezilla

We covered a lot of information today, and it may seem like a lot to take in if you're a beginner. For now you should concentrate on becoming comfortable with the following aspects of WordPress:

- Posts
- Pages
- Appearance
- Plugins
- Widgets
- Settings

Don't be afraid to play around with these a bit and get used to how they work. We'll be going into more detail on how to create pages and posts a bit later, as well as how to install plugins. WordPress is very easy to use once you familiarize yourself with its basic functions.

Day 4 – Enhancing WordPress

Now that you have a general understanding of how WordPress works and how to use its basic functions, we can concentrate on some of the intermediate/advanced functions of this platform. While WordPress is a very powerful platform right out of the box, these functions are going to help you take it to the next level.

We're going to cover how to install and use plugins, which plugins are best for your site, how to create and manage pages on your site, what security measure you should take to protect your site, and the basic on-site SEO you should be doing to make sure your site is indexed by Google and other search engines. While we will be going over less stuff today than we did yesterday, much of this will be more challenging and will require you to adequately understand what we went over yesterday.

Chapter 13 – Plugin Installation

The easiest and most popular way to enhance your WordPress site is to add plugins. As mentioned before, plugins are simply programs that you upload to your site that do different things. There are thousands of plugins available that do *many* different things. Before we get into which plugins are the best for your site, I'm going to walk you through how to install them.

Installing Through WordPress

The fastest and easiest way to install a plugin is through the WordPress control panel. To get started, click on the Plugins tab on the left-hand menu. The default page that opens will be the one showing your installed plugins. Click on the "Add New" subtab.

In the search box type "Google XML Sitemaps," then click search. A list of plugins will come up, and Google XML Sitemaps should be at the top or somewhere near it. This plugin basically helps search engines like Google and Bing to index your site easier.

Install Plugins

Search | **Search Results** | Upload | Featured | Popular | Newest

Keyword ⌄   google xml sitemaps   (Search Plugins)   *72 items*

Name	Version	Rating	Description
Google XML Sitemaps Details | Update Now	3.2.8	☆☆☆☆☆	This plugin will generate a speci search engines like Google, Bin better index your blog. With suc for the crawlers to see the comp retrieve it more efficiently. The p WordPress generated pages as Additionally it notifies all major s
Better WordPress Google XML Sitemaps	1.2.1	☆☆☆☆☆	With BWP GXS you will no long 50,000 URL limit or the time it ta generated. This plugin is fast, cc and can be extended via your ve

Click on "Install Now" and a window will pop up asking for confirmation. Click "OK" and the plugin will install. A new page will open up, and click "Activate Plugin" to activate the plugin.

Google XML Sitemaps
Activate | Edit | Delete

This plugin will generate a special XML sitemap whi engines like Google, Yahoo, Bing and Ask.com to b

Version 3.2.8 | By Arne Brachhold | Visit plugin site

Now the plugin is installed and activated. Google XML Sitemap's settings/options page is located in the Settings tab on the left. Because this plugin pretty much works the way it is supposed to right out of the box, you don't really need to configure it or mess with anything.

Many of these plugins will have an option for you to donate to the creator. Because the creator is giving the plugin away for free, it's always nice to support the plugin you like by giving a little back to the creator if you can. Even donating $1 can make a difference.

☐	**Google XML Sitemaps** Deactivate | Edit	This plugin will generate a special engines like Google, Yahoo, Bing Version 3.2.8 | By Arne Brachholc Support | Donate ⟵

Installing Plugins Using FTP and cPanel.

In addition to installing plugins through WordPress, you can also do it through FTP and cPanel, just like with themes. In fact, this is absolutely no different from how you do it when you install a theme, so I'm not going to go over this again. Here is the file path you will use, and the only difference is that you're going to put the plugin in the plugins folder, not the themes folder.

For Add-on Domains:

root folder/ → public_html → [the add-on domain name] → wp-content → plugins.

For the Root Domain:

root folder/ → public_html → wp-content → plugins

In most cases it is much easier and faster to install plugins through WordPress, but if you download a plugin from a website or if you buy one (not all plugins are free), you will have to use FTP or cPanel. Certain plugins don't show up in the WordPress plugins search, so downloading them then uploading them like this is a must in this case.

Chapter 14 – Recommended Plugins

With so many plugins to choose from it can be easy to end up installing a ridiculously huge amount on your site. While there is nothing wrong with having a lot of plugins, you can streamline things a bit by making sure you get the ones that are going to benefit you the most.

Also, the nature of your site will impact what plugins you choose. However, there are certain plugins that are practically essential regardless of what kind of site you're building. Here is a list of some of my recommended free plugins and what they do. The ones that I consider essential will be marked as such.

Zemanta

Zemanta is a plugin that actually installs into your browser and must be downloaded outside of WordPress. Despite this, Zemanta actually functions inside your WordPress control panel when you open the post page to edit or create a new post.

Zemanta provides you with content recommendations and allows you to easily add a variety of things to your post, such as pictures and related articles. It also allows you to easily create text-based links, and it recommends tags that you can add to your post just by clicking on them.

Click here to get Zemanta for free.
http://www.zemanta.com/

Automatic SEO Links

This plugin allows you to quickly and easily turn any word or phrase into a link in your text. It also allows you to set links to "nofollow" if you want, and it only links the first word in each post so your entire post isn't spammed up with links.

To configure it, check out the Automatic SEO Links subtab in the Settings area of the left-hand menu on the control panel.

This plugin can be found using the WordPress plugin search function and can be installed from there. Or you can get the plugin by clicking here. http://wordpress.org/extend/plugins/automatic-seo-links/

SEO Friendly Images

Images on your site can also be a great way to attract visitors through places such as Google Images and Yahoo Images. This plugin makes sure that the images on your site have the correct tags so that they are properly indexed by search engines. The options for this plugin can be found under the Settings tab in the control panel main menu.

SEO Friendly Images can be found and installed by using the WordPress plugin search function. Alternately, you can get the plugin by clicking here. http://wordpress.org/extend/plugins/seo-image/

SEO Tag Cloud Widget

If you plan to use a tag cloud on your site, you should definitely pick up this plugin. Tag clouds are sometimes not read correctly by search engines, but this plugin will ensure that your tag cloud is converted into an easily read HTML code so that search engines pick it up more easily.

You can find and install this plugin using the WordPress plugin search function. Alternately, you can get this plugin by clicking here. http://wordpress.org/extend/plugins/seo-tag-cloud/

SEO Title Tag

This SEO plugin helps to identify tags on your site to search engines so that they're better indexed and ranked. It can be used to add tags to your posts, pages, main page, and any URL that exists anywhere on your site. The options for this plugin can be found in the Settings section in the menu to the left.

SEO Title Tag can be found and installed using the WordPress plugin search option. You can also get it by clicking here. http://wordpress.org/extend/plugins/seo-title-tag/

Slick Social Share Buttons

There are a variety of ways to add share buttons for Facebook, Google +1 and more to your website, but this plugin makes it fast and easy. Slick Social Share Buttons creates a social share button bar that can be customized in a variety of ways and configured to show up on the pages you specify.

The best thing is that it scrolls with the page itself so that even when visitors scroll down it's still visible. To access the configuration options for this plugin, click the new tab that appears under Settings in the WordPress control panel main menu.

Slick Social Share Buttons can be found and installed using the WordPress plugins search function. Or you can click here to get it. http://wordpress.org/extend/plugins/slick-social-share-buttons/

Subscribe to Comments

This plugin is great for getting visitors to return to your website if you encourage comments. Subscribe to Comments allows visitors to subscribe to the comments section on your posts. When a new comment is added the visitor receives an email alert. This plugin is highly recommended for content-heavy sites and blogs. The options for this plugin can be found in the Settings tab on the WordPress main menu.

You can find and install Subscribe to Comments by using the WordPress plugin search function or by clicking here.

http://wordpress.org/extend/plugins/subscribe-to-comments/

Personal Favicon

This plugin makes managing your website's favicon (the little symbol next to the URL) incredibly easy. While this plugin may not be essential, it is **highly** recommended because your favicon is important for branding purposes. The options for this plugin will be located in the Settings tab in the WordPress main menu.

Personal Favicon can be found and installed using the WordPress plugin search feature. You can also get this plugin by clicking here http://wordpress.org/extend/plugins/personal-favicon/.

SEO Ranker Report

Manually keeping track of which pages and posts on your site are ranking well in Google can be a major chore. This plugin allows you to keep track of your website's posts and pages rankings based on keywords. In fact, you can configure this plugin to track data from any URL you want.

It should be noted, however, that many people using HostGator have been unable to get this plugin to work due to errors. The options for this plugin are found in their own unique tab that will show up under the Settings tab in the WordPress main menu.

You can get SEO Ranker Report by using the WordPress plugin search option or by clicking here http://wordpress.org/extend/plugins/seo-rank-reporter/.

WP-PageNavi

This plugin adds a stylish page navigation area at the bottom of your website that is fully customizable. If you run a blog or website that has many different areas and categories, this plugin can help make navigation a lot easier for visitors. The options for WP-PageNavi can be found in the Settings area of the WordPress menu.

This plugin can be found and installed using the WordPress plugin search function or by clicking here http://wordpress.org/extend/plugins/wp-pagenavi/.

Google Analyticator

This handy plugin allows you to check your Google Analytics data directly from your WordPress dashboard instead of having to go to Google Analytics to check it each time. While this isn't essential, it can save you a lot of time. The configuration options for this plugin can be found in the Settings tab on the WordPress main menu. Look for "Google Analytics," not "Google Analyticator."

You can get Google Analyticator by using the WordPress plugin search option or by clicking here http://wordpress.org/extend/plugins/google-analyticator/.

Breadcrumb NavXT

This plugin is great for optimizing your on-page SEO. It provides a link chain at the top of each post linking viewers back to where they came from. For example, if they are on a post titled "Dog Walking" in the category "Dog Behavior" the breadcrumb trail will read something like "Home → Dog Behavior → Dog Walking." This is also great for helping your viewers to navigate your site.

This plugin has a ton of options that you can customize and that can be found in the Settings tab in the WordPress control panel menu. I would recommend clicking the General tab and changing the Home Title to the actual name of your site. This will cause the word "Home" to be replaced in the trail with the name of your site, which is more SEO-friendly.

Breadcrumb NavXT Settings

| General | Current Item | Posts & Pages | Contact Form | Categories & Tags | Miscellaneous |

Breadcrumb Separator >
Placed in between each breadcrumb.

Breadcrumb Max Title Length 0

Home Breadcrumb ☑ Place the home breadcrumb in the trail.

Home Title: Home

Home Template `<a title="Go to %title%." href="%link%">%htitle%</a>`
The template for the home breadcrumb.

Home Template (Unlinked) %htitle%
The template for the home breadcrumb, used when the breadcrumb is not linked.

Something you have to keep in mind when using this, and the reason I didn't list this plugin as "essential," is that you have to insert some CSS code to get it to work in most themes. The code you use is:

```
<div class="breadcrumbs">
   <?php if(function_exists('bcn_display'))
   {
      bcn_display();
   }?>
</div>
```

In most cases this should be inserted in the Single Post (single.php) section of the Editor section in the Appearance tab of the WordPress control panel.

128

```
$adsize = get_option('flex_adsense_loc1size');

$adtype = get_option('flex_adsense_loc1type');
```

Documentation: Function Name... ▾ (Lookup)

(Update File)

(header.php)
headersearchform.php
ie6style.php
theme_options.php
Main Index Template
    (index.php)
legacy.comments.php
Page with no title Page Template
    (page-template-notitle.php)
Page Template
    (page.php)
Search Form
    (searchform.php)
Sidebar
    (sidebar.php)
simple_recent_comments.php
Single Post
    (single.php)
style.php
wp-pagenavi.php

Where you insert this code will determine where the navigation is displayed. I like to do it either above the title or just below the post date.

There are also ways to edit the code itself to change the font, make the trail appear in multiple places, and more, but doing so is different for each theme. If you are interested in doing this I suggest looking up resources on Google or in YouTube, depending on what theme you are using.

Remember, this can seem complicated if you have never done CSS. If you aren't confident that you can do this without screwing up your theme, either get someone else to do it, look up some tutorials on YouTube for help, or just don't bother with it.

You can get this plugin by using the WordPress plugin search function or by clicking here http://wordpress.org/extend/plugins/breadcrumb-navxt/.

WordPress Related Posts (Essential)

This plugin adds a list of related posts at the bottom of each post you create. This is great for SEO as well as encouraging visitors to visit multiple pages on your website, which is one of the keys to beating Google's Panda update. Just about any site imaginable can benefit from this. The options for this plugin will be found in the Settings tab and be listed as "Related Posts."

You can get WordPress Related Posts by using the WordPress plugin search function or by clicking here http://wordpress.org/extend/plugins/wordpress-23-related-posts-plugin/.

WP Super Cache (Essential)

Providing your visitors with a good user experience is another key to defeating Panda, and if your site loads really slowly you're going to be in trouble. This plugin helps to ensure that your website loads quickly regardless of how much traffic you're getting by keeping a cached version of your site in the browser. The options for WP Super Cache can be found in the Settings tab in the WordPress main menu.

You can get WP Super Cache by using the plugin search function in the WordPress control panel or by clicking here http://wordpress.org/extend/plugins/wp-super-cache/.

Google XML Sitemaps (Essential)

We already went over this one. Google XML Sitemaps generates a sitemap to help your website be indexed more easily by search engines like Google. No matter what kind of site you're building you *must* get this plugin. The options for this plugin can be found in the Settings tab on the main menu.

Google XML Sitemaps can be found and installed using the WordPress plugins search function or downloaded by clicking here http://wordpress.org/extend/plugins/google-sitemap-generator/.

All in One SEO Pack (Essential)

There are many SEO plugins out there, but this is probably the most popular free one. All in One SEO Pack works to help optimize each page and post, as well as your website as a whole. Just don't forget to configure it after you've installed it, or it will be functionally useless. The configuration options can be found in the Settings tab on the main WordPress menu.

All in One SEO Pack can be found using the WordPress plugin search option and installed through the control panel. Alternately, you can get the plugin here http://wordpress.org/extend/plugins/all-in-one-seo-pack/.

Contact Form 7 (Essential)

Regardless of what kind of site you're building, you're going to need to give your visitors a way to contact you. Contact Form 7 allows you to not only put a contact form on your Contact page (or anywhere you desire), it also allows you to edit and customize your contact form. The options for Contact Form 7 are listed in the plugins page under the plugin name and are labeled "Settings."

Contact Form 7 can be found by using the search function in WordPress and can be installed directly from the control panel. You can also get it by clicking here http://wordpress.org/extend/plugins/contact-form-7/.

Really Simple Captcha (Essential)

This plugin is recommended to keep bots from relentlessly spamming your email address through your contact form. This plugin adds a captcha form that visitors have to complete in order to contact you. Really Simply Captcha was developed by Takayuki Miyoshi, the same individual who created Contact Form 7, and is intended to work with it.

To get this plugin to work you have to go into the settings for Contact Form 7 and click on the drop-down menu that says "Generate Tag" and select "Captcha."

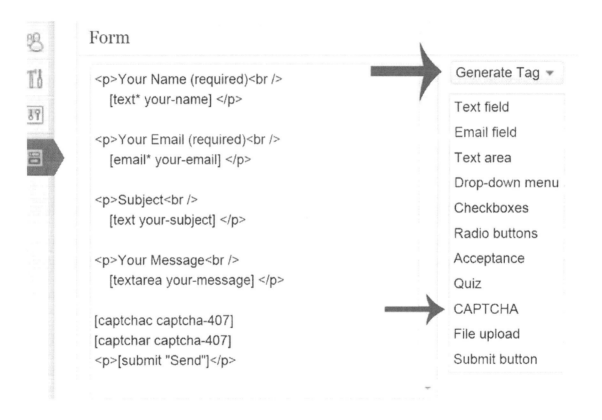

You then copy and paste the two bits of code at the bottom over into the field to the left just before the last tag.

Generate Tag ▾

CAPTCHA   ✕

Name

captcha-277

Image settings

id (optional)   class (optional)

Foreground color (optional)   Background color (optional)

Image size (optional)
☐ Small   ☐ Medium   ☐ Large

Input field settings

id (optional)   class (optional)

size (optional)   maxlength (optional)

Copy this code and paste it into the form left.
1) For image

[captchac captcha-277]

2) For input field

[captchar captcha-277]

133

```
<p>Your Name (required)<br />
   [text* your-name] </p>


<p>Your Email (required)<br />
   [email* your-email] </p>


<p>Subject<br />
   [text your-subject] </p>


<p>Your Message<br />
   [textarea your-message] </p>


[captchac captcha-407]
[captchar captcha-407]
<p>[submit "Send"]</p>
```

Really Simple Captcha can be found through the plugin search function on WordPress and can be installed from there. You can also get it by <u>clicking here</u> http://wordpress.org/extend/plugins/really-simple-captcha/.

Akismet (Essential)

Akismet comes already installed on WordPress and is a spam blocker. To activate it, you have to go to the plugin page, click "Activate," then click the link where you go to get your API key. There are paid versions with more options, but the free version is fine. Once you get the key, click the link in the yellow bar at the top on your WordPress control panel that prompts you to enter it. Once you enter the key you're good to go. Akismet will have its own configuration link in the Plugins tab on the WordPress main menu.

Choosing the Right Plugins

While some plugins work well with pretty much any site and are essential for good SEO, blocking spam, and other functions, your plugin selection will largely depend on the type of site you're creating. Some plugins are designed to enhance blogs, and others to enhance affiliate sites. Consider what functions you need on your site and choose your plugins accordingly.

Chapter 15: Creating Pages

One of the first things you are going to want to do on your WordPress site is to create several pages. While you can create as many pages as you want for whatever purpose you want, it is recommended that you start by creating an About page, Contact page, and Privacy Policy. Something to keep in mind about pages is that they will show up in your navigation bar unless you make them hidden, which I'll go over in just a moment.

About

Your About page is going to be the page where you explain a bit about who you are, what your site is all about, and any other essential info you feel your visitors need. Depending on the type of site you're creating, you may want to put a picture of yourself here, because having a picture of yourself will increase your trust and credibility among your visitors.

To create your About page, click the pages tab in the WordPress control panel and then select Add New. This will open the page creation page.

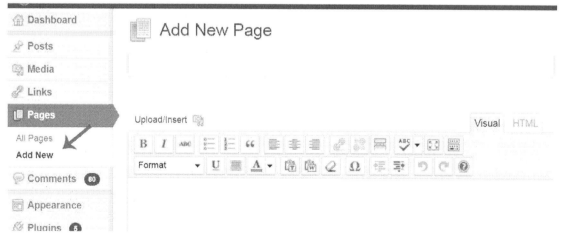

Creating a page here is as simple as adding a title, then entering the text you want. You can also add pictures if you need to by clicking the Add Media button.

When you're writing don't forget that you have access to a variety of tools in the text toolbar, such as bold, underline, block quote, add hyperlink, and more.

Also of note is the HTML tag. You can click this if you want to enter HTML information in your page, such as different fonts and text sizes. You can also use HTML to insert pictures that are hosted at a separate location.

Add New Page

If you are having trouble figuring out how to create your About page, click here http://www.lambertklein.com/about.html to take a look at mine and get an idea of how it should look and what info should be included. Remember, there is no set formula for your About page, just make it unique and suited to your site and your personality. It also pays to provide a contact link on your About page.

Once you have finished writing your page, you can do three things: save your draft to work on later, preview your page in a new tab or window, and publish your page immediately. I would recommend previewing your page before publishing, just to make sure it looks right.

Publish

Save Draft   Preview

Status: **Draft** Edit

Visibility: **Public** Edit

[::] Publish **immediately** Edit

Move to Trash   **Publish**

Visual   HTML

There are a few other things you can do before you publish your page, such as assigning a parent page or changing the template to remove the sidebar. For SEO purposes it is recommended that you leave the sidebar. This is especially true if you have advertisements in your sidebar.

There is also an option that says "Set Featured Image," which attaches a thumbnail image. This is practically useless for pages but can be useful for posts in some cases. It must be mentioned though that this feature doesn't work well with some themes, including the default Twenty Ten theme, thus requiring you to edit some CSS to make it work. If you are having trouble getting it to work with your theme, click here http://codex.wordpress.org/Post_Thumbnails to visit the WordPress support page on it.

Page Attributes

Parent

(no parent) ▾

Template

Default Template ▾

Order

0

Need help? Use the Help tab in the upper right of your screen.

If your theme supports it, then Featured Image button would show up here.

Contact

This is the page where you provide your contact information. It's completely up to you how much info you provide, but you should at least have a contact form, as mentioned previously. Don't forget to make sure your Captcha plugin is activated so you don't get flooded by spambots. Once the page is set up to your liking, preview and publish it.

Privacy Policy

Having a privacy policy is just standard procedure for most sites, and it would be wise to incorporate one into your site as well. Creating a privacy policy page used to be as simple as installing a plugin, but there are no longer any functional privacy policy plugins, to my knowledge. Instead what you can do is search Google for privacy policy templates to use instead.

For a generic template that works with just about every website click here http://www.inixmedia.com/2010/03/free-privacy-policy-sample-template-for-a-new-website/. Just be sure to edit certain parts of it to suit your particular site.

To create a more customized privacy policy you can go to www.freeprivacypolicy.com. This site will allow you to create a highly customized privacy policy for free, but you're going to have to go through some stuff to get it.

You will have to input your email address once you create the policy, then you will be shown some upsells. These are unnecessary, and I don't encourage you to buy these unless you really need them for some reason. You will then be emailed a username and password as well as a link allowing you to access your privacy policy. It will be in both text and HTML, so you can enter it either way when you create this page.

Overall, www.freeprivacypolicy.com is a great way to get a very customized privacy policy for free as long as you're willing to put up with the fact that they're going to put you on their mailing list and try to sell you a bunch of stuff.

Sneeze Pages

A sneeze page is simply a page that has links to multiple posts on it. It could be titled something like "Hottest Articles," "Breaking News," or "Most Popular Blog Posts." The purpose of a sneeze page is to drive visitors deeper into your site, because most won't bother clicking on your Archives section in the sidebar if you use one.

Also, while sneeze pages are great, you can also incorporate sneeze page elements into other sections of your blog. For example, you could create a "sneeze widget" that features some of your most popular posts in the sidebar. You can also configure your excerpts on the main page to feature two or three links in addition to the thumbnail and description, turning them into mini sneeze pages in a way.

The thing to remember about a sneeze page is that you want to give it a really catchy, interesting title. No one is going to click on a sneeze page or widget if you label it something like "Older Posts." Make the title interesting like the examples given earlier.

Other Pages

Depending on what type of site you're creating, you may want to add other pages as well. If your site is based on selling a service, you can add a page to describe different aspects of it. If you're selling products, you can have a different page for each product category. The possibilities are endless, and ultimately it's up to you to decide what pages you need to create.

Two types of pages that you may need to consider are a Terms of Service page and a Terms of Use page. These are useful if you're running a business (such as a membership website) directly from your website and visitors need to be aware of certain things.

Parent and Child Pages

If you're creating a website in which you're going to have multiple pages listed under the same category, you can assign them to a parent page. In a way this functions somewhat similarly to how you would assign posts to a post category.

A good example of this would be if you want to group your Privacy Policy, Terms of Service, and other legal pages together in your navigation bar. What you would do is create the page that you want to be the parent page first, then as you create your other pages, you would select the option to assign them to your first page as a child page. You can find this feature by scrolling down and looking on the right side of the screen in the page creation page.

One thing to keep in mind is that the parent/child page system is **not** to be used to replace the categories/posts system. This is because you want your categories to appear in the sidebar for SEO. The parent/child page system should really only be used to save space on the navigation bar.

Hidden Pages

Sometimes you may want to have pages on your website that are hidden. A good example of this is a download page where people who purchase your products go to make their downloads. You obviously don't want this on the navigation bar, or people will be downloading your products for free.

There are two ways to create hidden pages. The first is relatively simple and involves using FTP to upload the page to your add-on or root domain folder, depending on which one you're using. The only drawback to this is that you have to use HTML to create the page in the first place. If you're going to do this, I would recommend using an HTML editor such as nvu. You can get nvu for free by clicking here http://net2.com/nvu/download.html.

There is also a bit of code you will need to add in order to make sure that these pages aren't indexed by search engines like Google. The code is

```
<meta content="nofollow,noarchive,noindex"
name="robots" />
 <meta content="never" name="revisit" />
```

This typically goes right below the </title> tag.

```
1.  <!DOCTYPE html PUBLIC "-//W3C//DTD XHTML 1.0 Transitional//EN" "http://w
2.  <html xmlns="http://www.w3.org/1999/xhtml">
3.  <head>
4.    <meta content="text/html; charset=utf-8"
5.    http-equiv="Content-Type" />
6.    <title>Thank You!</title>
7.    <meta content="nofollow,noarchive,noindex"
8.    name="robots" />
9.    <meta content="never" name="revisit" />
10.    <link type="text/css"
11.    rel="stylesheet" href="style.css" />
12.  </head>
13.  <body>
```

Also make sure that you give the HTML file a unique, hard-to-guess name like "Special-Offer-Download83925783275" or something like that so people won't be able to figure out how to get to it easily.

Another thing you must be aware of when doing this is that in addition to the HTML file, you must also upload any CSS style sheets and images associated with the HTML. These all go in the domain name folder with the HTML file.

In any event, if you use FTP the file path will be "root/ → public_html → domain name folder" for add-on domains and "root/ → public_html" for the root domain.

If you want to hide pages you create in WordPress the easy way, simply search and install the PC Hide Pages
 http://wordpress.org/extend/plugins/pc-hide-pages/
plugin from the WordPress Plugins section. This will not only make selected pages hidden but also hide them from search engine spiders. This will ensure that they aren't indexed and can't be accessed through Google and other search engines.

Another option if you want to keep pages off of your navigation bar but still public is the plugin Exclude Pages. You can click here
http://wordpress.org/extend/plugins/exclude-pages/
to get this one.

Creating a Static Home Page

The main page of your website can come in one of two different varieties: Static and Latest Posts. By default your home page will show your latest blog posts, and if you decide to go with this format make sure that you are using the "Insert More Tag" button to show only an excerpt on the home page. You're also going to want to limit how many posts are shown by clicking Reading under the Settings tab in the main WordPress menu.

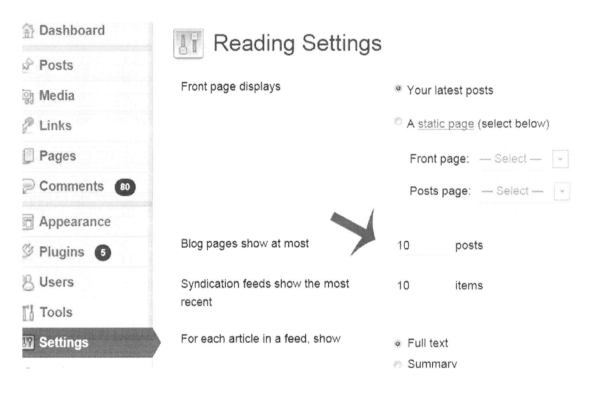

To create a static home page simply click on Reading in the Settings tab and take a look at the page that opens. The first thing on the page is two bubbles. The first is "Your latest posts" and the second is "A static page." Select the second one to make your home page a static page.

Now what you have to do is go down to the drop-down menu below and select which page you want to be your static home page. The page that you select will then be listed as "Home" in the navigation menu on your website. You also need to select what page your posts will be displayed on.

![icon] Reading Settings

Front page displays   ○ Your latest posts

                                       ◉ A static page (select below)

                                          Front page: Sample Page ▾

                                          Posts page: — Select — ▾

Blog pages show at most   10   posts

Syndication feeds show the most   10   items
recent

Whether or not you have a static home page is completely up to you. However, if you're creating a blog it is usually best to keep your latest posts as the home page.

147

Chapter 16: WordPress Security

One of the worst fears of anyone who runs a website is having their site hacked. This can lead to lost data, corrupted files, Trojans, and malware entering your computer and many other undesirable outcomes. The good news is that protecting your WordPress website isn't hard as long as you employ smart online and offline security practices.

Limiting Access

As with many things, prevention is the key when it comes to protecting your WordPress site. As we touched upon earlier you shouldn't be accessing your WordPress site from public computers if you can help it, and you should certainly never set your username and password to "remember" for any public or shared computers.

It is also a good idea to make sure you log out of your WordPress account once you're done using the control panel if you use a shared computer. This will prevent anyone else from gaining access by using your cookies. This is also highly recommended if you access your control panel using a mobile device or phone that could potentially fall into the wrong hands.

Computer Vulnerabilities

All the WordPress security in the world isn't going to do you any good if your computer is infected with malicious software or compromised by a hacker. Make sure your computer always has the latest antivirus and malware protection available, and make sure that it is always up to date. Also ensure that you perform scans regularly. Remember, anyone who gets into your computer can potentially get into any of your online accounts such as WordPress, Facebook, and more as well as your WordPress sites.

Updating WordPress

WordPress.org's built-in security is pretty robust, but like any security system it must be updated regularly, or new and improved malicious software can get through. Make sure that you regularly check the control panel of your WordPress sites so that you can update them as soon as an update becomes available.

Web Server Vulnerability

If your hosting server becomes compromised then your WordPress sites are as good as compromised as well. The good news is that practically every hosting company out there has exceptional security features. However, you have to do your part too.

Avoid logging in to your cPanel from public computers, and always log out on shared computers just like you do for your WordPress control panel. Changing your password frequently can also be a good idea.

Keep in mind that if you are on a shared server (most web hosting plans fall into this category unless you specifically get dedicated hosting), your data can be more easily compromised. Luckily most big companies like HostGator and Bluehost have excellent security measures.

If you purchase reseller hosting (from a private individual, not a web hosting company), you need to speak with the server administrator beforehand to make sure that you understand what security measures are in place and what precautions you should take. This is especially true if the reseller hosting is from a lesser-known company.

Overall, protecting your web server is actually more important than protecting your WordPress site itself. This is because if someone gets into your hosting, they could gain access to every site stored on that hosting server, which could lead to catastrophe.

Network Vulnerability

If you are on a LAN or are part of a cloud computing network, make sure you are familiar with the security systems in place. While most cloud computing companies have ultra-secure networks, LANs and other public computing networks may not. This makes it very easy for your passwords and other sensitive information to be intercepted. Don't access your WordPress account or web hosting account if you are unsure of a network's security level.

FTP Vulnerability

FTP presents another possible security breach because it accesses your server directly. Many FTP clients, such as Filezilla, can be configured so that you must input a password in order to access a server by configuring separate profiles for separate web servers. This is a must on shared computers. Also, Quick Connect absolutely should not be used on shared computers, because anyone can access servers that have been typed in previously if you forget to delete the history.

Also, FTP clients should not be used while connected to networks with anything less than exceptional security, because your entire server data will be exposed when you access the hosting server. This could lead to a sever compromise by someone on the network or an external computer.

File Permissions

Some files on your WordPress site are write accessible by your web server. What this basically means is that your web server can access these files and alter them. In some cases this is necessary for the function of your website, but certain files should never be write accessible. Here is a quick list of files that you should make sure are only writeable by your user account.

- The root directory (except .htaccess if you want WordPress to automatically configure rewrite rules for you)
- /wp-admin/
- /wp-includes/
- /wp-content/plugins/

It should be noted that /wp-content/ itself should be writable.

You can change file permissions directly from your hosting server through your cPanel in most cases, or you can use an FTP client to do it as well. In Filezilla you can do this by accessing your server and bringing up the file you want to change permissions for. Right-click the file and select "File Attributes." A little window will pop up with your permissions. Make sure that "Write" for Group and Public is disabled, then click OK. Do this for all the files above and any others you don't want to be rewritable.

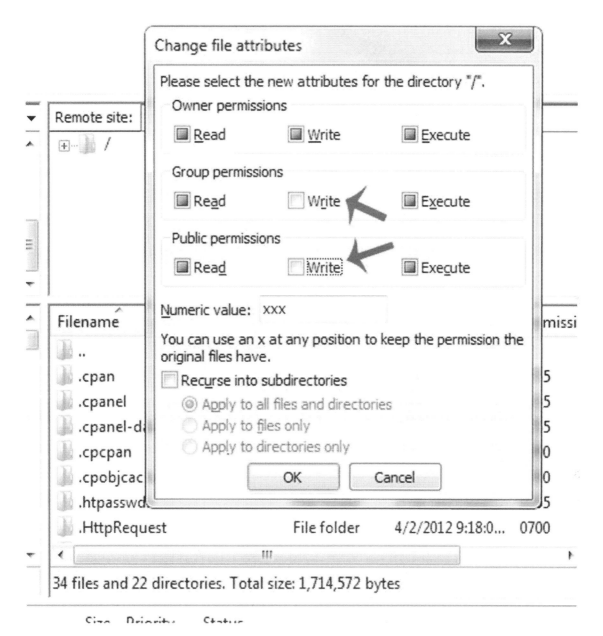

Firewall Plugins

You can further deter potential hackers by installing firewall plugins on your WordPress site. While this can be overkill in many cases, considering WordPress already has very tight security, you can still do it if it will help you feel better about your website's security.

WordPress Firewall 2
http://wordpress.org/extend/plugins/wordpress-firewall-2/
and cloudsafe365_for_WordPress
http://www.cloudsafe365.com/how-it-works/
are two popular firewall options.

Plugins that Need Write Access

There may come a time when you download a plugin that says it needs write access to files that you have disabled write permissions for. In this event you need to make absolutely sure you trust the plugin publisher and that it isn't going to do anything malicious to your system. If you are unsure about the plugin, check the code to make sure it doesn't contain anything threatening, or get someone who understands code to check it for you.

SQL Database Security

If you are going to have multiple WordPress sites, a good security measure is to install each one on a different database managed by a different "user." What I mean by user is the fact that when you create a database you have to create a user profile that will be identified by a username and password. This will ensure that if someone does hack into one of your WordPress sites they won't automatically have access to the others.

You create a database by going into your hosting account and creating what is known as a MySQL database for each additional WordPress site you want to install. While I can't do a walk through for every single hosting company out there, I will briefly walk you through how to do this on HostGator so you can get an idea of how this is done.

First go into your cPanel and select the icon that says MySQL Database.

Databases

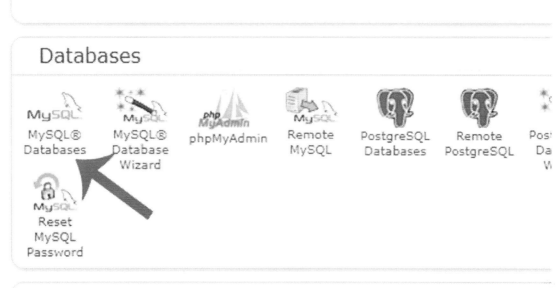

Software/Services

Enter the database name, then click "Create Database." Now you will have to create a user for the database by entering a username and password below.

Create New Database

New Database: lambertk_Test ✓

Create Database

MySQL Users

Add New User

Username: lambertk_ NewUser ✓

Password:

Password (Again):

Strength (why?): Very Weak (0/100)   Password Generator

Create User

Once that is complete you're going to have to add that user to the database. Remember, you can add a single user to multiple databases, but that would defeat the purpose because you want each WordPress site to be managed by a different username and password.

To add a user to a database, simply select the user you want from the drop-down box and the database you want from the drop-down box under it, then click "Add."

Create User

Add User To Database

User: | lambertk_NewUser ▾ |

Database: | lambertk_Test ▾ |

| Add |

A new screen will pop up prompting you to give permissions. It is recommended that you give all permissions to the user by clicking the box at the top that says "All privileges." Once you're done click "Make changes."

Another way you can do this is to use the SQL Database Wizard, which you may find easier.

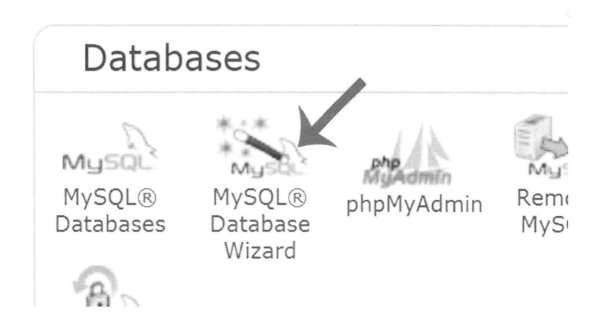

Once this is done you now have a database that you can install your WordPress site on. This is somewhat technical but isn't hard at all. What you first need to do is locate your wp-config.php file for your WordPress site. Once again you can use either an FTP program or your cPanel. The file path will also be different for the root domain and add-on domains.

Important: Do not confuse wp-config.php with wp-config-sample.php that is located directly above it.

Root Domain Path:

root/ → public_html (you then have to look in the subfiles for this folder)

Filename	Filesize	Filetype	Last modified
.htaccess	246	HTACCESS...	8/31/2012 6:29:...
index.php	395	PHP Script	8/31/2012 2:57:...
license.txt	19,929	Text Docu...	8/31/2012 2:57:...
readme.html	9,177	HTML Doc...	8/31/2012 2:57:...
sitemap.xml	2,035	XML Docu...	9/1/2012 2:38:3..
sitemap.xml.gz	698	GZ File	9/1/2012 2:38:3..
wp-activate.php	4,264	PHP Script	8/31/2012 2:57:...
wp-app.php	1,354	PHP Script	8/31/2012 2:57:...
wp-blog-header.php	271	PHP Script	8/31/2012 2:57:...
wp-comments-post.php	3,522	PHP Script	8/31/2012 2:57:...
wp-config-sample.php	3,177	PHP Script	8/31/2012 2:57:...
wp-config.php	3,519	PHP Script	3/23/2012 9:36:...
wp-cron.php	2,726	PHP Script	8/31/2012 2:57:...
wp-links-opml.php	1,997	PHP Script	8/31/2012 2:57:...
wp-load.php	2,341	PHP Script	8/31/2012 2:57:...
wp-login.php	29,084	PHP Script	8/31/2012 2:57:...
wp-mail.php	7,712	PHP Script	8/31/2012 2:57:

Add-on Domain Path:

root/ → public_html → [the name of your domain] (you then have to look in the subfiles for this folder)

Remote site:	/public_html/blog

- **?** ajxlightbox4_files
- **?** ajxlightbox5_files
- **?** ajxlightbox6_files
- **?** ajxlightbox_files
- **?** bin-dl
- **blog** ←
- **?** cam

Filename	Filesize	Filetype	Last modified
.htaccess	246	HTACCESS...	8/31/2012 6:29:...
index.php	395	PHP Script	8/31/2012 2:57:...
license.txt	19,929	Text Docu...	8/31/2012 2:57:...
readme.html	9,177	HTML Doc...	8/31/2012 2:57:...
sitemap.xml	2,035	XML Docu...	9/1/2012 2:38:3...
sitemap.xml.gz	698	GZ File	9/1/2012 2:38:3...
wp-activate.php	4,264	PHP Script	8/31/2012 2:57:...
wp-app.php	1,354	PHP Script	8/31/2012 2:57:...
wp-blog-header.php	271	PHP Script	8/31/2012 2:57:...
wp-comments-post.php	3,522	PHP Script	8/31/2012 2:57:...
wp-config-sample.php	3,177	PHP Script	8/31/2012 2:57:...
wp-config.php ←	3,519	PHP Script	3/23/2012 9:36:...
wp-cron.php	2,726	PHP Script	8/31/2012 2:57:...
wp-links-opml.php	1,997	PHP Script	8/31/2012 2:57:...

Once you have accessed the right folder, right-click the wp-config.php file and open it in a text editor if you're using FTP. If you are using your cPanel, you will edit the file in a new browser tab or window in most cases.

There are three sections of this file you need to edit: DB_NAME, DB_USER, and DB_PASSWORD. Simply change these values to your database name, username you created for it, and the password you created when you made the SQL database earlier.

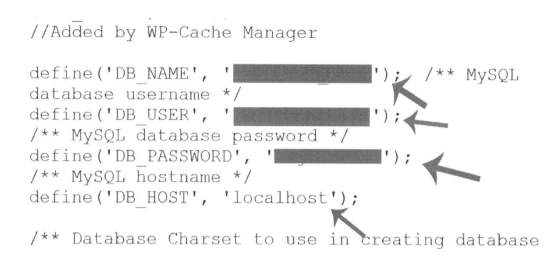

```
//Added by WP-Cache Manager

define('DB_NAME', '               ');    /** MySQL
database username */
define('DB_USER', '               ');
/** MySQL database password */
define('DB_PASSWORD', '          ');
/** MySQL hostname */
define('DB_HOST', 'localhost');

/** Database Charset to use in creating database
```

Once you have changed the data, save the file. Now your site will be attached to the database. Keep in mind that in some cases you may be prompted to install WordPress once again when you try to visit the site or login page in your browser. Just fill in the required information and WordPress will be ready to be used again.

It is recommended that you do the editing of the wp-config.php file through FTP so that you can save a copy of this file to your computer before you begin editing. This way if you screw something up you can delete the messed-up file and upload the original. You can then try again.

Keep in mind that a WordPress site should be installed on a new database before you begin doing any work on it. This is because a new database will have no data on it. If you create a new database for an existing WordPress site and edit the wp-config.php file, the old data will remain in the database that was automatically created when you first installed WordPress. The original database will usually be something like "[your webhosting log in name]_wrdpr1" or "[your web hosting login name]_wrdpr2."

If you have multiple WordPress sites already created, you can simply check their wp-config.php file to see which databases they are each connected to. You can then add a unique user and password to each instead of having to create a brand new database for each one. This will allow you to keep your data and not have to rebuild each site from the ground up.

Back Up Your Data

In the event that your WordPress site or host server becomes compromised, you want to ensure that your data is backed up. Backing up your data regularly can be a great way to prevent a catastrophic loss of data if you are compromised. There are several plugins that can help you back up your data, such as Online Backup for WordPress http://wordpress.org/extend/plugins/wponlinebackup/ and EZPZ One Click Backup http://wordpress.org/extend/plugins/ezpz-one-click-backup/.

You should also back up your SQL Databases if you are using multiple databases for multiple sites. This can help to protect against data loss as well.

Monitoring

If you really want to stay on top of things, you can actively monitor your website's logs for hacking attempts, your files for any suspicious changes, and even use a web-based integrity monitor to monitor your site externally. This level of security can be somewhat complicated to those who are unfamiliar with how these things work. Fortunately, you don't usually need to go so far as to constantly monitor your files and data for intrusion attempts, so long as you're smart about your website and server security.

Stopping Spam

When it comes to blocking spam in your comments section, Akismet is the most preferred spam-blocking plugin. It comes with WordPress, but you have to go to their site to get the API key, as mentioned in the plugins section.

To keep your contact form from being spammed, make sure you're using a captcha plugin. Really Simple Captcha is recommended, especially if you are using Contact Form 7.

Chapter 17: Website SEO

SEO for your website is incredibly simple yet also one of the most important things you're going to have to do to ensure that your site ranks well in the search engine results. Let's go over the key components of website SEO.

Domain Name

The domain name of your website is where your SEO begins, as we discussed earlier. Your domain name should preferably be a keyword phrase that has a high search volume, low amount of competition, and be composed of two to three words. This will help to ensure that the search engine spiders that crawl your site understand what it is about, and rank it accordingly. Also, because your root domain shows up on every single page and post of your website in the URL, it's one of the most powerful forms of SEO for your site as a whole.

Title and Tag Line

Your title and tag line show up by default in your WordPress site's header. When you install a custom header they disappear for most themes, while with some themes you will have to set your configuration to not show them. The thing to remember is, just because they aren't visible in your header doesn't mean they aren't important.

You can set your title and tag line by going into the Settings tab on the control panel menu and clicking on "General."

⚙ General Settings

Site Title	⟶	Kindle and PDF Books
Tagline	⟶	Internet Marketing Books
		In a few words, explain what this site is about.
WordPress Address (URL)		`http://www.lambertklein.com/blog`
Site Address (URL)		`http://www.lambertklein.com/blog`
		Enter the address here if you want your site homepage to ￰
		installed WordPress.
E-mail Address		stuff@1thinkhealthy.com
		This address is used for admin purposes, like new user no

Make sure that both your title and tag line contain the same keywords as your domain name or related keywords. Because this is technically a part of your header, whether they are visible or not, your title and tag line will be showing up on every page and post as well.

Meta Tags

Meta tags are another way to help search engines recognize what your site is about and rank it accordingly. The easiest way to do meta tags is to use the All in One SEO plugin mentioned earlier. It will allow you to enter information such as your home page's title, description, and a list of related keywords.

I enjoy this plugin and have made a donation:	☐
Plugin Status:	◉ Enabled ○ Disabled
Home Title:	Kindle and PDF Books
Home Description:	Internet Marketing Books
Home Keywords (comma separated):	wordpress,books,pdf,kindle,inte
Canonical URLs:	☑
Rewrite Titles:	☑
Post Title Format:	%post_title% | %blog_title%

This is a great way to optimize your home page for search engines. All in One SEO also allows you to do this for individual pages and posts, but we'll get into that a bit later.

Breadcrumb Navigation

As mentioned before in the plugins section, having breadcrumb navigation on your site is a great way to appeal to the search engines by basically adding even more keywords to each post in the form of navigation links. Additionally, this improves the internal linking structure of your site, which appeals to the search engines as well.

As previously mentioned though, getting breadcrumb navigation plugins such as Breadcrumb NavXT to work can be a chore, depending on what theme you're using. If you are having trouble getting breadcrumbs to work with your theme, search online for resources that can help.

Sitemaps

A sitemap is basically a map of your site formatted in a way that is appealing to crawlers that the search engines use to index websites, posts, and pages. This aspect of SEO can be easily taken care of by installing the Google XML Sitemaps plugin.

Tag Cloud

A tag cloud is a widget that is displayed on your site that lists all of your most common tags. There has been somewhat of a controversy over whether or not tag clouds help SEO, and whether or not you should use them at all. Generally speaking there is nothing wrong with using tag clouds, so long as you don't overdo it. Having too many tags in the tag cloud can appear as "keyword stuffing" and have a negative effect on how search engines rank your site.

Another thing about tag clouds is that while they do enhance the internal linking structure of your site, they do it in a somewhat random way. This gives you practically no control over what pages and posts your "SEO juice" is going to.

If you do choose to use tag clouds, make sure you're using a plugin such as SEO Tag Cloud Widget to assure that your tag cloud is easily read by search engines. Also make sure that you are placing your tag cloud down at the bottom of your sidebar so that you aren't taking up space that could be used for other purposes, such as opt-in forms or advertisements.

WWW Redirect

There is an issue with search engines counting the www version of your URL and the non-www version as two separate pages. This can lead to duplicate content issues, which could cause your site to be penalized in the search engines.

To correct this problem, simply go into your Settings and go into "General." Now set your Site Address (URL) to http://www.yourdomain.com. This will ensure that all non-www versions are redirected to the www version.

Day 4 Recap

Here is what we went over today.

- How to install plugins through WordPress
- How to install plugins using FTP
- Plugins can also be installed through your cPanel
- Recommended plugins
- How to create pages
- How to create hidden pages
- How to create child pages
- What pages are commonly used (Privacy Policy, etc.)
- How to protect your WordPress account and web server from being compromised
- How to back up your data
- How to use SQL databases to protect multiple websites on the same server
- How to stop spam
- How to optimize your on-page website SEO

Some of the things we discussed today were relatively simple and straightforward, whereas others were much more complex. For certain tasks that depend on what hosting company you're using and what theme you have installed, I would once again suggest looking up resources using Google and YouTube. From this point forward I will assume that you have downloaded and installed all the plugins I listed as essential.

Day 5 – Content Creation

Thanks to what you learned yesterday and the day before, you should now have your WordPress site not only set up but also enhanced with plugins, essential pages, categories, a good theme, and any security precautions you wanted to take. Basically the only thing your site should lack at this point is content and a monetization method.

Today we're going to cover adding content to your site as well as how to do proper SEO for your posts and pages. We'll also discuss how to handle your comments section and provide a good user experience for your visitors. All in all, today should be a very short and easy day for you.

Chapter 18: Creating Posts

The majority of the content that you add to your site will be done by creating posts. This allows you to create web pages on your site that contain text, images, video, and even audio files. You also have the option to set the posts you create to be published at a later date if you'd like. There are many different things you can do on the post creation page.

Understanding the Posts Page

Creating posts on WordPress is incredibly easy. Just click on the Posts tab in the control panel menu, click "Add New" and you will bring up the post page.

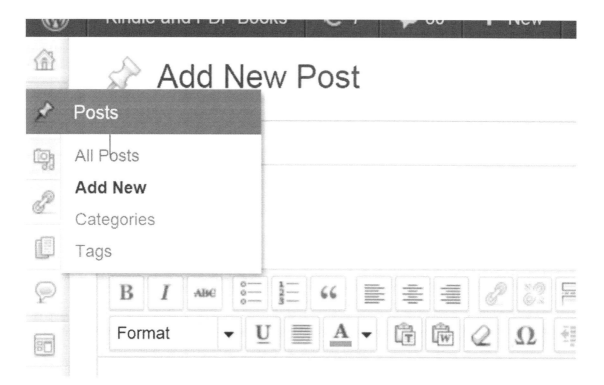

Here you will enter your title and any content you want in the text area. Keep in mind that there are two ways to view the text area, Visual and HTML. Visual is great for most posts you'll be making, while HTML is generally only used to enhance your post in various ways, such as changing the font or text size.

There are also several buttons available on the toolbar here. Most are self-explanatory and will say what they do when you mouse over them. Block quote is a feature that allows you to select a portion of text to appear in a gray block (depending on your theme) while italicized and indented. The gray block won't show up in the text editor here, you'll have to either preview or publish your post to see it. That is, if your theme is capable of showing it.

The Insert More Tag is an incredibly handy feature that allows you to insert a line that cuts off how much of your post will show on the main page of the site if you have your blog posts as the main page. It used to be that you'd have to do some complicated CSS stuff or download a plugin to do this, but now you can do it from the post editor.

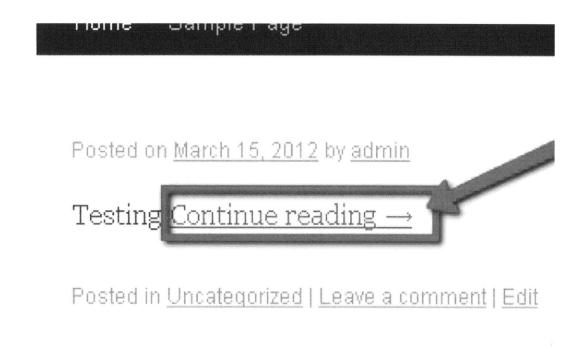

The Kitchen Sink button can be clicked in order to show additional options on the toolbar. Click it again to hide the extra options.

Upload/Insert

The "Paragraph" tab will allow you to choose some formatting options such as headers and default text, and "Align Full" will adjust the alignment of your paragraphs so that they look better.

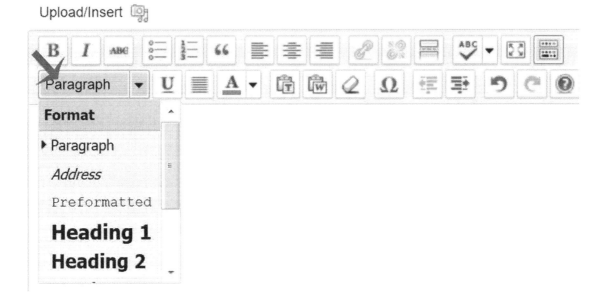

You will also find options that allow you to paste in plain text as well as text from Microsoft Word. This can be handy if you prefer to type out your posts in MS Word first. Keep in mind that your formatting options will not be kept when you do this.

Also available here is a custom character button that allows you to insert symbols such as © if you want. You can also use the indent and out-dent buttons to mimic the effect of a tab key.

Once you have created your post there are several things you can do. If you look to the right you will see a few different options to choose from. "Publish" immediately allows you to publish your post, "Preview" gives you the opportunity to see what your post will look like, "Save Draft" will save the post as a draft, and "Move to Trash" will move the post to the trash can.

Publish

Save Draft   Preview

Status: **Draft** Edit

Visibility: **Public** Edit

Publish **immediately** Edit

Move to Trash   **Publish**

There are also options to change the status, visibility, and the date. Click on "edit" to open these. The status of a post can be set to Draft and Pending Review. Draft will allow you to come back and edit the post later while Pending Review is good for allowing you to check over posts that have been created by hired help if you outsource your content creation before publishing them.

"Visibility" allows you to set who can and can't view your post and to stick the post to the front page if you wish. Generally speaking, "Public" will be your choice here. The "Password Protected" option can be great for making posts and areas of your site that are only accessible to certain people. This is particularly useful if you have a special paid membership section on your site.

Publish

Save Draft   Preview

Status: **Draft**

Draft ▾   OK Cancel

Visibility: **Public**

◉ Public
  ☐ Stick this post to the front page
○ Password protected
○ Private

OK Cancel

🗓 Publish **immediately**

09-Sep ▾ 01 , 2012 @ 20 : 21

OK Cancel

The date allows you to either publish your post immediately or set a time for it to be published in the future. This is good for situations in which you want to drip-feed content to your viewers. When you come back to edit a post that has already been published, you can use this option to edit the date the post was published.

Visibility: **Public**

◉ Public

☐ Stick this post to the front page

◎ Password protected

◎ Private

(OK) Cancel

Before you publish your post you're going to want to do a few things first. Scroll down and you will see All in One SEO below the text box. Take a moment to enter your title, description, and keywords in the fields. This will drastically improve your SEO for the post.

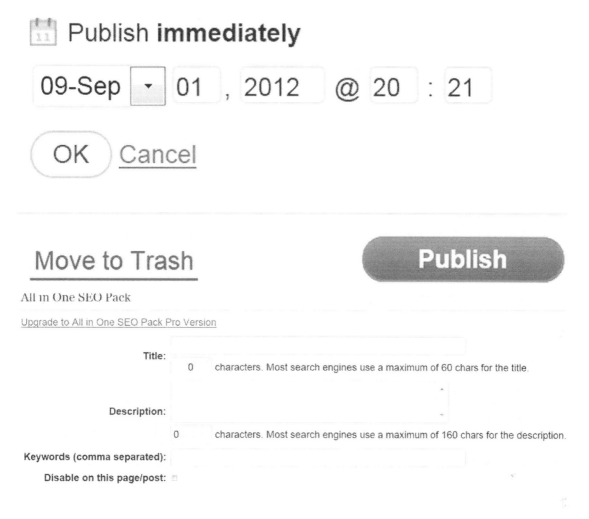

Next scroll down further and look to the right. You'll see boxes that allow you to choose your categories and set your tags. You can choose from categories and tags that already exist or create new ones if you feel the need.

Categories

All Categories	Most Used

☐ Internet Marketing Books

+ Add New Category

Tags

(Add)

You may also want to add a media file to your post, and that's where the Add Media button comes in. Clicking it opens a box that allows you to drop files in or browse your computer for them. Once you've uploaded a file you can then access it in the Media Library tab. An alternate way of doing this is to click the "From URL" tab. This will allow you to link in a media file from an external source.

→Upload/Insert 📷

| **B** | *I* | ~~ABC~~ | ☰ | ☰ | " | ☰ | ☰ |

| Format ▼ | U | ☰ | **A** ▼ | 📋 |

Add Media

From Computer   From URL   Media Library

Add media files from your computer

(Select Files)

You are using the multi-file uploader. Problems? Try the browser uploader instead.

Maximum upload file size: 10MB. After a file has been uploaded, you can add titles and descriptions.

Once you have a media file uploaded, or have selected one from an external source, you can edit how the file displays. For SEO purposes, you should set the title and alternate text to keywords that have to do with the image and post you're creating. You can also fill out a brief description, which is also good for SEO if you put your keywords in it. If you add a caption, it will display underneath the picture. The title will display when someone mouses over it once your post is published.

Once you've entered that information, select the alignment and size of the image. You may have to play around with this a bit to get it just right.

(Edit Image)

Title   *   appleImage2

Alternate Text

Alt text for the image, e.g. "The Mona Lisa"

Caption

Description

Link URL   http://www.lambertklein.com/blog/wp-content/uploads/2012/09/

(None) (File URL) (Attachment Post URL)

Enter a link URL or click above for presets.

Alignment   ○ ■ **None**   ○ ■ **Left**   ○ ■ **Center**   ○ ■ **Right**

Another feature of the Add Media function is that if you click on the button again after adding a picture, you will see a new tab labeled "Gallery." This tab will allow you to check out recently added images and the title and other information you gave them.

Once you have inserted as many pictures as you want and your post is 100% complete, click the preview button to see how it looks. If everything is fine, click the publish button to publish your post on your website. That's all there is to creating posts.

As you can tell, this is very similar to how you create pages but with a few extra options. Try playing around with this a bit until you get the hang of creating posts.

Formatting

When you create a post to publish online you have to take several things into account. First of all you need to understand that people online have *very* short attention spans. To deal with this you need to ensure that your content is broken up into short, easy-to-read paragraphs. If visitors see a huge block of text when they click on one of your posts, they're going to hit the back button pretty fast.

Also break up sections of your posts with bolded subheadings, similar to the way I do things here in this guide. People online tend to scan, not read, and bolded subheadings and bullet points will give them something to lock on to and focus their attention on.

Also keep in mind that up to 50% of your visitors may not even scroll down the page when they click on a post. This makes it imperative to have any important links "above the fold" in your posts.

When it comes to adding pictures to your posts, don't overdo it. Pictures should be used to enhance a post, and using too many will just be a distraction. If a picture doesn't have a clear purpose, then it doesn't belong in your post.

Chapter 19: Content SEO

When you create content for your website you also want to make sure that it is SEO optimized so that it will be picked up by the search engines. You see, not only are your website's main page/URL crawled by search engine spiders and ranked, but your individual posts and pages are as well. This makes it important to have good SEO on each page and post.

It is unwise to build sites centered around just one keyword, because of the debut of Google's Panda update. You should make your posts centered around keywords that are related to the keyword you used in your domain name. For example, if your domain is "dogtraining.com" your posts could target keywords such as "dog obedience classes," "dog walking," and more. It also pays to do good keyword research to ensure that you're targeting high search volume/low-competition keywords.

Your Title

For pages, don't worry about the title. It should be created for ease of user navigation, not SEO. For posts, however, you do need a good SEO title. This means writing a title that not only includes your keywords, but also makes use of copywriting techniques. Copywriting is the art/science of getting people to take action. In this case, it means clicking on your title when your posts come up in the search engines.

Several examples of title elements that get clicks online are:

"How to…"
"The Secret of…"
"5 Powerful Ways to…"
"The Top 10 Best Cures for…"

Here are some examples of complete titles that get clicks:

"7 Ways to Cure Gout Fast!"

"The Secret to Getting Your Ex Back! Guaranteed!"
"The Top 10 Songs of 2011"

"Warning! Could Your Tap Water Be Deadly?"

"3 Dirty Psychological Tricks to Date Any Girl"

"5 Ways Your Cable Company is Scamming You!"

To fully understand the art of writing titles for the web that get clicks, I recommend going to Copyblogger.com
http://www.copyblogger.com/.
 You can click here
http://www.copyblogger.com/magnetic-headlines/
to view a page that deals specifically with this topic.

You actually can add an SEO-friendly title to a page by using All in One SEO. Just make the main title field at the top navigation friendly, and then enter a keyword and SEO-friendly title in the All in One SEO box below the text field.

Also, you may have heard something about "H1" tags and things like that. On WordPress your post/page title counts as the H1 tag. If you want you can also add an H2 or H3 tag in your post, but this is not necessary and won't have that big of an impact on SEO.

Keyword Density and Placement

Years ago it used to be that the more keywords you had in your posts, the better, and this led to what was known as "keyword stuffing." These days, keeping your keyword density at around 1% to 4% is fine in most cases. In fact, if your density for a keyword is too high, Google will actually penalize you for that.

In addition to density, you also need to have your keyword in certain areas of your post. The most important is the first sentence. This is because the first sentence or two is going to be used in the description of your post when it appears in Google and other search engines, causing them to place more emphasis on this area.

Some people also claim that it helps to have your keyword bolded as well, and it certainly doesn't hurt, especially if you are including it in an H2 or H3 tag. Italicizing your keyword can help too. Just make sure you're not overdoing it with the formatting, because you don't want your post to look ridiculous with tons of bolded, italicized, underlined, and highlighted words.

While each post should center around one main keyword, you should also sprinkle in several related keywords. This is known as LSI and is used by Google search algorithms. For example, if the main keyword for your post is "dog walking" you could add in words like "dog training," "dog breeds," "dog collars," "leashes," "obedience," and more. Generally speaking, these related keywords should happen naturally as you write your content.

Picture SEO

Using the WordPress Media options, you can give your pictures titles, captions, and descriptions, as we discussed earlier. If you're going to add pictures, take the time to make sure you're doing this for each of them, as the search engine crawlers do check images in addition to text, after all. This also gives them a better chance of showing up in places like Google Images, which can lead to additional traffic.

As mentioned before, the SEO Friendly Images plugin can help boost your picture's impact on your website's SEO.

Related Posts

Using the WordPress Related Posts plugin, you can have each post link to several other related posts. The links will be listed down at the bottom, and this is great for both SEO and internal linking structure. Additionally, it also encourages your visitors to visit additional areas of your site and spend more time on your site, two important factors for beating Panda.

Tags

Tags are simply a way of helping search engine crawlers to identify what your site is about and rank it accordingly. Keywords related to your site are the best tags to use, of course.

When you create a post, add tags but don't overdo it. Also don't forget to use All in One SEO to add keyword tags.

Chapter 20: Getting Comments

If your website is set up like a blog, or another content-heavy type of site, you want to encourage user participation as much as possible. The more visitors that interact on your site the better, and one of the main ways to get people involved is by allowing them to leave comments on your posts.

The thing is, in many cases people may not care enough to leave comments on your posts, regardless of how well written they are. Statistically speaking, 90% of viewers are "lurkers" and don't participate at all. Only 9% will occasionally comment, and only about 1% of visitors will actually comment on a regular basis. Here are some techniques you can use to encourage people to post comments on your site.

Tell Visitors to Leave Comments

The most straightforward method of getting people to comment on your posts is to simply tell them to. Most people don't want to bother thinking for themselves, and if you actively tell people to comment on your posts you'll increase the number of people who do in most cases.

Giving Visitors an Incentive

Sometimes to get people to comment you have to give them a bit of an incentive. Try having a contest in which the person who leaves the most unique, helpful, or insightful comment gets a free gift or something special. It could be a free mini report, a free copy of an eBook you have, or maybe a small gift certificate if your site is an online store or Amazon affiliate site.

Another method of rewarding people who comment is praising them. You can do this simply by leaving a comment of your own and telling someone that you enjoyed their comment, or by quoting their comment in another post. If you really want to go the extra mile, you can even email the person and let them know how much you enjoyed their comment.

Don't Make Visitors Log In to Comment

People online don't like to jump through hoops to do something, and that applies to leaving comments as well. Most visitors will not even register, let alone comment on your site, if you expect them to do this. Make sure you keep your comments section as easy to use as possible so that it appeals to a wider range of people.

Mind Your Behavior

Something that can turn off lurkers and keep them from leaving a comment is the fear of being called out by you publicly. Never lash out at your commenters or visitors, and always appear humble and friendly. If people think that there is a possibility of your going ballistic on them for leaving a comment, fewer people will comment.

In the event that a commenter calls you out on something or flames you, don't retaliate. If you made a mistake own up to it, and if you didn't simply ignore the flamer or block them. Also be aware of people who may try to troll you in the comments, which is to say, intentionally provoke you. It can be hard to spot a troll at times, but if you think someone is trying to make you mad on purpose don't fall for their tricks.

Good Moderation

If you want people to comment on your posts, make sure that your comments section is kept clean and civil. While there is nothing wrong with people expressing alternate opinions, it can get out of hand if people start flaming one another and being rude in general. Keeping your comments section under control will encourage more people to participate.

Ask Questions

Another great way to get people to comment is to ask readers a question at the end of your post and direct them to leave their answers in the comments section below. This almost always works to help you get more comments because people like to appear knowledgeable.

Interact with Your Visitors

You can comment on your own posts, and this is a great way to interact with your readers and converse with them. This will also signal to lurkers that you are willing to respond to comments and answer any questions they may have. Try to make sure you respond to at least one comment per post you make.

Start a Forum

If you notice that your site is getting a ton of activity in the comments sections on your posts, you may want to consider creating a forum so that your readers will have a more organized area where they can chat with one another and interact with you personally.

There are several plugins that allow you to create a forum on your WordPress site, with WP-Forum Server being one of the most popular http://wordpress.org/extend/plugins/forum-server/.
Other popular choices are bbPress
http://bbpress.org/ and Simple:Press
 http://simple-press.com/.

Chapter 21: User Experience

When you create content for your website you want to focus on creating a positive user experience for all of your visitors regardless of what kind of site you're building. First and foremost your content needs to be useful and provide value to your visitors. Not only will this encourage repeat visits, but it will also make your site look good in the eyes of Google and other search engines.

Every time you create a post or page make sure you ask yourself: Is this useful to the visitor? You want to provide as much value as possible but without "giving away the store" if you are selling something. There are different strategies for this for different models of monetization, and we'll get into that in a bit.

Zemanta

One way of enhancing your content is by using the plugin Zemanta that we went over earlier. This plugin is interesting because it installs into your web browser but functions in your WordPress control panel when you create a post or page.

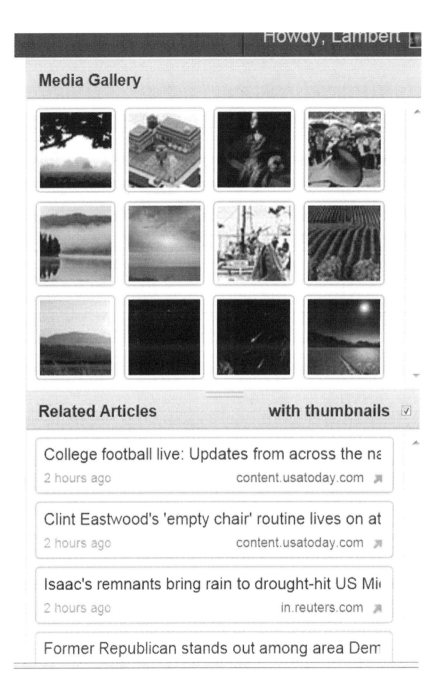

Zemanta is basically a content suggester, or rather, it suggests additional content to supplement what you've already written. For example, if you write a post on dog training, Zemanta will suggest pictures, related articles, and keywords that are related to dog training. It even allows you to turn certain keywords in your post into links to external content sources. If you're focusing on keeping visitors on your site, you may want to skip that option, but if you do use it you should ensure that the link opens in a new tab or window so that visitors don't navigate away from your site.

Videos

Another great way to enhance the user experience on your site is to add videos. Not only does this provide useful information and/or entertainment to your visitors, it also keeps them on the site longer, which is another key factor to beating Panda.

To upload a video, simply click the Add Media button we talked about earlier and select the file you want to upload. Once it has loaded you will have the option of entering a title, caption, and descriptions, all of which you should do for SEO purposes. Keep in mind that the video will be inserted as a link that opens the video on another page, not as an actual video on your post.

Thankfully there are plugins that allow you to post actual videos in your posts and pages. One of the most popular is called Secure HTML5 Video Player. This can be found using the WordPress plugin search function or by clicking here http://wordpress.org/extend/plugins/videojs-html5-video-player-for-wordpress/.

Once the plugin is installed you can use it by inserting some code into your posts. The first step is to upload a video into your WordPress media library like we just discussed. You will also need to upload an image to use as the cover image for the video. Taking and saving a screen cap of the video is a good way to do this, just make sure the dimensions are set to around the same values that you'll be using when you post the video or else the image will be skewed.

Once you have the video and image ready to go, copy their URLs into WordPad or another document, because you will need them later.

Now that you have everything ready, paste this code into your post where you want the video to go. You can paste it in the Visual or HTML section of the text editor, as either one is fine. The parts that say "video domain name" and "image domain name" are where you enter your video and image information.

[video mp4="video domain name" poster="image domain name" preload="yes" autoplay="no" loop="no" width="640" height="264"]

You may have to alter the width and height to fit the dimensions of your blog. There are also other bits of code and ways of creating this code that can be found in the HTML5 Video Player configuration section, which can be found under the Settings tab in the WordPress main menu.

Embedding YouTube videos in your site is a bit easier. Simply go to YouTube, find the video you want, and click on "Share." A new menu will open. Now click on "Embedded" and you will get an HTML code. Take this code and enter it in the HTML view of the text editor in the post or page where you want the video to appear. You can edit the height and width if you need to as well.

198

After making your selection, copy and paste the embed code above. The code changes based on your selection.

FAQ and Help Pages

We've already talked about Privacy Policy, Terms of Service, and About pages, but there are other pages you can add to create a more positive user experience. If you find you're getting a lot of questions that cover the same topics, you can create a FAQ page to help explain things to your visitors.

If your site is complex and has a lot of ways for users to interact with it, you may need to create a Help Page. A Help Page will have a list of links to information on a variety of topics that users may have trouble with. This is typically only necessary if your site is highly technical in regards to user interaction.

Social Media Links

Regardless of what kind of site you are creating, you're probably going to want to include social media links. These links allow visitors to share your content with others by clicking Facebook, Google +1, Twitter, and other buttons that you install on your site.

One plugin that we talked about that helps you do this is Slick Social Share Buttons. There are other plugins that provide a similar function, of course, and ultimately it doesn't really matter which one you use, so long as you get the share buttons on your site in a conspicuous, easy-to-see location.

One great location for share buttons is at the end of each post. This gives readers who enjoyed your post a chance to share it on their favorite social networks.

Opt-in Form

If you are going to be building an email list as a form, or just to keep in touch with your viewers, you need an opt-in form and autoresponder. Popular choices include Aweber, Mail Chimp, and Imnica Mail. Because this is a form of monetization, we'll get into it a bit more later.

http://www.aweber.com/
http://www.mailchimp.com/
http://www.imnicamail.com/

Day 5 Recap

This is what we went over today:

- How to create a post
- How the text editor works
- How to add images and videos to posts/pages
- Proper SEO for posts and pages
- The importance of copywriting for post titles
- The proper way to format your posts for an Internet audience
- What Zemanta does
- How to get visitors to leave comments

⚔ A few key ways to enhance the visitor experience on your site

Today was pretty basic. Content creation isn't hard at all, and there isn't much to adding video and images to your posts either. The most important thing we discussed today was how to properly format your content and how to write compelling titles.

We also briefly touched on the topic of user experience. This is very important, especially when it comes to beating Google's Panda update. I'll get more into that later when I go over how to not only beat Panda, but how to make it work in your favor.

Day 6: Monetization and Traffic

Most of you reading this guide are probably thinking of monetizing your WordPress site somehow, even if you are just creating a blog. While there are many different ways to monetize your website, they are functionally useless if you don't have traffic.

At this point not only should you have a fully functional WordPress site, but you should also have a good idea of how to create compelling, user-friendly content. All that's left now is to monetize your site and drive traffic to it, and you're in business. Today we'll be going over exactly how to do that.

Chapter 22: Monetization

Monetizing your website can be a great way to not only earn passive, or nearly passive, income but to also drastically increase your site's value. You can keep the site forever as a money maker or sell it off for a big pay day. Generally speaking, the more money your site makes, the more you can sell it for.

There are several ways to monetize your site, and the layout, theme, and overall design of your site will be greatly dependent on which methods you are using. Don't forget that you can mix and match monetization methods and aren't obligated to stick with just one.

Google AdSense

AdSense is a program you join that allows you to post AdSense ads on your website. When visitors click these ads, you receive a commission. The commission you receive depends on the ad, but most get you anywhere between $0.10 and $0.50 on average. As you can tell this isn't a lot, so you're going to have to make up for this by getting a ton of people to click those ads.

AdSense sites are primarily content oriented. For example, you could create a site on the different types of cat litter boxes and provide articles and blog posts related to that. AdSense will detect that your site is about litter boxes, if you've done proper SEO like we've talked about, and post ads related to litter boxes and cats in general.

When you create an AdSense site there are several factors you need to take into consideration to be successful. You need to make the site about something that is very specific and preferably something people would be willing to spend money on. Your ad placement also needs to be top-notch, because setting up your ads in the right places will lead to higher conversion rates. There are themes that are specifically designed for this, and we'll discuss those later.

Another thing you have to understand about AdSense sites is the way the content should be written. Because your goal is to get your visitors to click your ads, you don't want your content to be quite as interesting or easy to read as you would on a normal website. While your content should still be useful, don't bother with bolded subheadings, bullet points, or anything else that can possibly distract from the ads. In fact, longer, blockier paragraphs can actually work to your advantage in this situation so long as you don't cross the line and have massive blocks of text.

Ad Rental

Another method of generating money using ads is offering to rent ad space on your site. If you're getting a lot of traffic, people will come to you and ask to do this most of the time. If not place a banner or page on your site's home page that mentions your ad rental.

When you have an ad rental program you can go about charging your clients in several different ways. You can have a system set up in which they are charged a set price, or you can have potential clients make you an offer. Either way is viable. Typically payment will be set up on a recurring basis. In some cases you may want to offer longer subscriptions at a discounted rate, such as a 1-year subscription at 30% off, so you can get more money up front.

To be successful with this method of monetization, you have to understand the value of your site's traffic. By checking out your analytics you can determine which pages get the most traffic and therefore which pages are worth the most to clients. You should charge more for premium ad space like this while charging less for ad space that isn't as hot. You can also use your analytics data to help advertise your ad rental program by showing potential clients exactly how much traffic they can expect.

Two areas where you should always charge a high amount for ad space are your header/top feature and your sidebar. This is because ads in your header/top feature and in your sidebar will show up on every single page. This makes them extremely valuable.

The best thing about an ad rental program is that it can be combined with practically any other monetization method. Pretty much the only time it's ill-advised is if you are trying to make sure there are no traffic leaks in the event that you're selling affiliate products or your own products. For example, if you're selling an eBook on how to cure gout and a client wants you to put an ad on your site advertising a free report on how to cure gout, that would be an obvious traffic leak and conflict of interest that you would want to avoid.

Affiliate Sites

An affiliate site is one dedicated to selling products as part of an affiliate program. This can take many different forms, such as Amazon reviews sites, single-page sales letter-style websites, and blogs that offer tips and information on things related to the products, then link to the products in a resource box at the end.

While affiliate sites can be very profitable, there are some things to consider. First of all, you need to make sure you're joining a good affiliate program that pays you a reliable and decent commission. Second, you need to make sure that the content on your site is very highly focused and leads visitors to the logical conclusion of buying the products you're promoting. For example, if you have a site that sells throwback football jerseys, you need to make the content on your site about throwback football jerseys, not just football in general.

The last thing to remember about affiliate sites is that your content should focus on a presell, not a hard sell. This is because in most cases you will be linking to a sales page of some sort created by the owner of the products, so leave the selling to them. Your job is to just get your visitors to click through and go to the sales page.

Getting visitors to click your affiliate links requires the use of strong calls to action. You should be using deliberate phrases such as "Click Here for More Info on How to Cure Your Gout Today!" Also be sure to include a healthy dose of hype, big promises, and generally just give them a huge incentive to click your links. You can also use the element of scarcity by mentioning limited time offers and the element of curiosity by saying something like "Click Here to see the Unlikely Cure for Gout that Revolutionized the Medical World!"

Remember, with an affiliate site, the quality of your site is, is only half the battle. If the owner of the affiliate program has a terrible sales page that doesn't convert, it doesn't matter how good your site is. Scout your affiliate program's landing page and sales pages to make sure they're not amateurish garbage before joining an affiliate program.

Selling Your Own Products

Selling your own products is a great business model for a WordPress site. The only catch is that unlike an affiliate site where you simply direct visitors to an affiliate offer, you actually have to create the products yourself. These products can be eBooks, videos, MP3s, and more.

While you will have to work harder to promote your products, the major advantage here is that each product you create becomes an asset that you own for the rest of your life. This opens up a ton of new possibilities and allows you to use your products in a variety of ways, such as selling them in online bookstores, breaking them up and giving them away as part of a membership site, or giving a mini product away to get people to join a mailing list.

Out of all the ways to monetize your website, this is perhaps the most versatile and can be combined with other monetization methods very easily. The only downside is that it definitely takes more work.

Email Marketing

Regardless of what kind of monetization method you're using on your site, you should also incorporate list building. For example, if you have an AdSense site and you put an email signup form on it, people who click your ad will only be worth between $0.10 and $0.50, while people who sign up to your list can be marketed to over and over again with larger-paying offers.

To build a list you need an autoresponder, which is a piece of software that helps you organize your list, send out timed messages, and create opt-in forms. As mentioned before, popular autoresponders include <u>Aweber</u>, <u>Mail Chimp</u>, and <u>Imnica Mail</u>. Some autoresponders are free while you have to pay for others.

Another important thing to remember is that a list of buyers is worth much more than a list of freebie seekers. While it is acceptable to get people onto a list by offering them a freebie, you want to follow up with a paid offer as soon as possible. Those that accept the paid offer should then be moved onto a separate list, your buyers list. You can then present paid offers to your buyers list more frequently and get a better response.

Also keep in mind that some autoresponders can be configured so that when someone buys a product of yours they are automatically signed up to your list. This is a great way to build a list of buyers right off the bat.

If your site focuses on list building exclusively, you are going to want what is known as a squeeze page. A squeeze page is a website layout that is configured for nothing more than getting people to sign up to your list. A typical squeeze page consists of an opt-in form and maybe a short blurb as to why someone should sign up. Sometimes a video is used instead of text. In any case, you need to make your offer extremely compelling and straight to the point.

Regardless of how you set up your site, you need to always have your opt-in form above the fold, because many visitors don't bother to scroll down. Your opt-in form should also preferably be in the header/top, or in the sidebar so that it appears on every page. Not every visitor to your site will hit the home page first, after all.

Service Arbitrage

This is an incredibly clever way to monetize your site. This consists of finding a good service online that is sold for relatively cheap, such as website building, content writing, or something of that nature. What you then do is configure your site to center around this service and advertise it. When people place their orders with you, you get the other service to actually do the work for you.

Here is an example of how this works.

Let's say you find a web design service that builds WordPress sites for $40 a site. You can then make your website advertising WordPress site construction for $80. When people place their orders you get the other service to do this and make a $40 profit.

You can even take this one step further by combining multiple services into one. For example, let's say you build a site offering total web development services. You can outsource the site construction, content creation, SEO, and other tasks to individual services that do these things and make a profit off of each transaction.

The main thing to watch out for here is making sure that the services you're getting to do the work for you are quality services that are reliable. For example, while many people on Fiverr do offer quality work, they sometimes disappear without warning. If this happens you need to be able to replace these people as quickly as possible. Also, as a rule it pays to hire each service beforehand in order to get a firsthand look at the kind of work they do, how long it takes them to do it, and their customer service skills.

Testing

There are many ways to monetize your website and there is no "best" way to do it. Additionally many of these methods can be combined with one another. To get the most out of your site it can be a good idea to test different methods and different combinations of methods to see which ones bring in the greatest amount of revenue.

For example, once you have a decent amount of traffic, you can promote affiliate products on your site one week then promote a pure AdSense site the next. Changing the monetization methods on your site does take a bit of work but isn't terribly time consuming. In the end it can be worth it to figure out which methods work the best for your niche and marketing style.

Residual Income

Something you always want to be focusing on with your monetization is residual income. Setting up your site and the monetization method so that it puts money into your bank account with as little effort as possible is key to building your business, because it frees up more of your time so that you can concentrate on expansion.

For example, if you can get your WordPress site to pay a portion of your monthly bills, you can cut back on your work schedule and focus on building more sites or exploring other business opportunities. Once you reach a certain level of residual income you'll even be able to begin pumping that money back into your business and be able to hire virtual assistants to handle most of the day-to-day tasks associated with maintaining and building your websites.

The key to bringing in a substantial residual income is optimization and outsourcing. On every site you build you want to streamline your monetization method so that you're bringing in the maximum amount of money for a minimum amount of time spent working on the site. This is especially important when hiring people to build and maintain your websites, because it will increase their productivity, ensuring that you're getting more for the money you're spending on hiring them. In the end, you want to get things to where you are personally doing as little work in your online business as possible.

Your Site Is an Asset

When you create a website, that website becomes an asset. How much your site is worth depends on two main factors: how much money it earns and how much traffic it gets. Obviously the amount of money it earns is the more important of these two factors and will have the greater impact on how much you can sell your site for.

Another thing to consider is that when you're building multiple sites your revenue tends to fall under the Pareto Principle, which says that 20% of your assets will earn you 80% of your income. This basically means that most of your sites will be underachievers while a select few will be superstars.

To make the most of the Pareto Principle, you should be building up and expanding upon your sites that do well and selling off your sites that underperform. While you may not get much for an underperforming site, you can still make some money by selling it on Flippa, which is preferable to hanging onto the site and paying its yearly domain fees in many cases.

Flippa is the world's most popular place for selling and buying websites. Generally speaking, you can sell a site on Flippa for 6 to 12 times what your site makes in a month. Obviously the longer the site has been around, and the more consistent the income steam has been, the more people will be willing to pay for it. This is a great way to unload unwanted sites or even get a huge payday by selling one of your superstar sites.

Just remember, on Flippa you should be using Escrow for all transactions over $1,000. There are scammers out there who will try to rip you off through PayPal by doing charge backs. Don't let this happen to you, and play it safe with all large transactions.

Chapter 23: Generating Traffic

All the monetization in the world isn't going to do your site any good if you can't drive traffic to it. The simple fact of the matter is that traffic = money. How much money is of course decided by how well optimized your site is and how targeted the traffic you're sending is to your monetization method.

Identifying Your Target Audience

This is something you should do before you attempt to direct any traffic to your site. Having a ton of traffic is practically useless if it's cold and untargeted. You want traffic that is highly targeted and preferably consisting of buyers, if you're selling products or a service.

Identifying your target audience isn't hard and consists of having an in-depth understanding of your niche. For example, if you are in the "cure snoring" niche you should do some research to determine who is most affected by snoring problems. Is it white males aged 20 to 30? Hispanic females aged 35 to 50? These questions and more need to be answered. Dig down deep and get specific data that will help you develop a mental image of the perfect customer for your offers.

Targeted Traffic

Once you understand who your target audience is, you need to figure out where they hang out online and how to get links to your website in front of them. A good example of this is Facebook. The Facebook crowd tends to be of the younger generation, so if the offers you have on your site appeal to this audience you could post ads on Facebook using their ad program. Alternately you could also create a fan page specifically to promote your website. For example, if you're going with the "stop snoring" niche you could make a page centered around that.

The key to getting targeted traffic is to make your traffic generation methods as specific as possible. If the offers on your website relate to the Chicago Bulls, don't target basketball fans in general, target Bulls fans. The principles of attracting targeted traffic should be applied regardless of what traffic generation method you're using. Getting 10 targeted visitors to go to your site is more valuable than getting 50 untargeted visitors.

Google AdWords

AdWords is a system of paid advertising offered by Google that displays your ads on the right side of the page when someone does a Google search. They have some strict regulations, but if you're willing to play by the rules you can generate a lot of targeted traffic very quickly. This can lead to huge payoffs in a relatively short amount of time.

The only downside to AdWords is the fact that it's a PPC (pay-per-click) system that charges you for every person who clicks on your ads. This can add up very quickly, and if your site isn't converting you can expect to lose a lot of money very fast. This makes in-depth testing and understanding of the AdWords system important if you want to be successful.

Facebook and More

AdWords isn't the only PPC system out there. Facebook and other sites have paid advertising programs that allow you to display ads as well. This can be incredibly effective if you have a good understanding of what kind of traffic a website is getting. For example, if your website is selling cat products and you discover another site that is all about cats, posting an ad on that site can be beneficial if it's getting decent traffic.

Many sites out there that get good traffic don't have official ad programs, but you can rent advertising space if you ask them. When negotiating, try to get them to present you with a price first so that you will be in a better position to haggle it down.

The #1 rule of using these methods of traffic generation is testing. If an ad isn't working, pull it, recreate it, and try again. If you just can't generate traffic from a particular site no matter what ad you use, stop advertising on that site, because there is no need to waste your money on it.

Paid Traffic Services

There are many services on the Internet that will send you traffic for a price. These services use a wide variety of different methods to send traffic to your website and most are pretty reliable.

The thing to keep in mind, though, is the fact that not all of these services send targeted traffic. In many cases, services such as these can send you thousands upon thousands of visitors in a short amount of time, but if the traffic isn't targeted it's not going to be worth your investment.

Do your research and make sure that the company you're going to be doing business with is reputable and does a good job of sending targeted traffic. Ask around and see if you can find people willing to refer or recommend a paid traffic service that they've had good experiences with.

Google Traffic

Traffic from search engines such as Google is known as organic traffic. The key to getting organic traffic is to rank high for your keywords, and that way when someone does a search for those keywords, your site is the first one to pop up in the search results, or is at least on the first page.

To rank high in Google and other search engines, the SEO on your website is very important, as we discussed. However, off-page SEO is going to be even more important.

Off-page SEO consists of backlinks that fall into three major categories: High Authority, Social, and Low Authority, ranked by importance in that order. High

Authority links come from sites/web pages with high page authority and high domain authority, which you can check using SEOmoz. Getting links from these sites can be challenging, but you typically only need around five per month to do well.

Social links come from social networking sites such as Facebook, Reddit, and others. These links are very easy to get and you generally only need around 15 per month.

Low Authority links come from article directories, forums, blogs, Web 2.0, and other similar sources. These links are also very easy to get, but for them to count you're going to need around 50 a month.

When it comes to establishing a linking strategy, don't simply have all your links point to the main page of your website. Disperse your links and have them target a variety of pages on your site, with your most popular, high-converting sites taking top priority. It obviously makes sense to post more links to the pages that make you the most money.

All of these links combined will serve to push your website, and its individual pages and posts, up the rankings in Google. It may take a bit of time to see results, depending on how much competition you have to overcome. Generally speaking, if you see two sites on Google Page 1 for a keyword that have both their domain authority and page authority less than 40, you shouldn't have trouble getting on Page 1 relatively quickly with good SEO.

How targeted search engine traffic is completely depends on your keyword selection. For example, "Buy Samsung Galaxy S2" is extremely targeted (and buyer targeted, which is a plus) while "Samsung Tablets" is significantly less targeted. This isn't to say you can't be successful with fewer targeted keywords, it will just negatively impact your conversion rates, which means you will need more traffic to make a decent amount of money.

Forum Marketing

Forum marketing is, as its name suggests, marketing to forums. The way to do this is to do a few Google searches to find highly targeted forums that have to do with your niche. For example, if your niche is "cat aggression problems" you should look for forums that deal with that or at least have subforums that deal with that topic. Forums that cater to animal or pet lovers in general would do you no good, however, because they would not provide targeted traffic.

One thing you have to remember when doing forum marketing is that most forums do not allow you to blatantly advertise your website and try to sell stuff. Make sure you familiarize yourself with each forum's rules before you begin marketing on them.

Some forums allow you to have a link in your sig to your website, while others allow you to have a link in your profile. When setting these links always make sure you're linking people to your pages/posts that have the highest conversion rates so that you make the most money.

Another rule of thumb when doing forum marketing is to present yourself as an expert in your niche and offer true value to the forum. Try going around and answering people's questions and making useful posts that give tips related to your niche. This will build up your credibility and get more people to click your links and actually buy from you when they get to your site.

Social Networks

One of the great things about social networks such as Facebook, Twitter, and others is that they allow you to both promote your website and create a good number of backlinks at the same time. Every time you create a new post on your website you should also create a post on as many social networking sites as possible. There are services such as OnlyWire (http://onlywire.com/) and plugins that can help make this task a lot simpler.

When creating social network posts, you must make your posts as interesting as possible. Give them good copy written titles, make the descriptions as exciting as possible, and even incorporate images if you feel the need to. Also, don't forget that many of these sites allow you to tag your posts, allowing you to determine what keywords it will come up for in searches on the network.

As with forum marketing, always give top priority to your pages and posts that are converting the best. While spamming is a good way to get banned from a social network, there is nothing wrong with promoting a high-converting page on your site one or two times a week.

Also don't forget that interaction is a huge part of social networks. If someone comments on your post, make sure you respond to them. This will make you look less like a bot and more like a real person. This will build up your credibility and help you to get more clicks in the long run.

Web 2.0

Sites such as Squidoo and HubPages are known as Web 2.0. Sites such as these allow you to create your own pages quickly and easily, and are a great way to reach a larger audience when driving traffic.

The largest benefit of using Web 2.0 is that they already get a lot of love from Google and other search engines. By picking and choosing your keywords wisely, it isn't hard to rank high in the search engine results. Ranking Squidoo posts, HubPages posts, and other Web 2.0 posts, in addition to your own website's pages and posts, can be a great way to really dominate a certain keyword and take over multiple slots on Page 1. This can lead to a sizable increase in traffic.

Also, don't forget that when you create these Web 2.0 pages you need to have very strong calls to action to get visitors to click through to your website, in addition to having a keyword-rich, copy written title. Proper on-page SEO is also a must, and make sure you have at least one call to action above the fold.

220

The biggest drawback to Web 2.0 is the fact that there are usually ads placed on your page that you have no control over. This can create a traffic leak in many cases. Also the fact that you don't actually have ownership of these Web 2.0 posts and pages that you create prevents them from being true assets.

While Web 2.0 is effective if used correctly, it can be time consuming to create multiple posts using these sites. This is a task that should be outsourced if you can afford it.

Article Marketing

Contrary to many Internet rumors, article marketing isn't dead, it just functions much differently these days. Instead of mass submitting articles to a ton of low-level directories, you should focus on submitting extremely high-quality, highly targeted articles to top-level directories like EzineArticles and others with the intent of getting your articles syndicated.
http://www.ezine.com/

When your article gets syndicated it's published on other websites, allowing you to take advantage of the traffic that the site gets. For example, if you published an article on stopping cat aggression it might get picked up and posted on a site about cats that gets a lot of traffic.

To make the most of this you need to hone your resource box writing skills. Your resource box is a little area at the end of your article that convinces readers to click on links to your website. Making use of copywriting techniques such as scarcity, big promises, curiosity, and very strong calls to action are a must to get a good click-through rate.

While submitting your articles to a lot of different directories isn't as effective as it used to be, it can still help you reach your 50 low authority link quota each month if you're having trouble doing it in other ways. To make this easier on

yourself I'd recommend picking up some software, like <u>ArticleBot</u>, to help with this, or outsource article submission entirely.
http://www.articlebot.org/

Something else that should be said about article marketing is that you don't want your articles on article directories competing with your website's content. To avoid this you should always post content on your site first and make sure it is indexed before posting it to an article directory. Alternately, you can just create fresh content to submit to article directories.

The Traffic Formula

Once you start getting some traffic you can begin to do rough calculations of how much money you're going to be making per month. The formula is as follows:

Search Volume + Conversion Rate + EPA = Income

For example, if you get 100 visitors a day, have a 3% conversion rate, and make $10 per conversion, you'd be making $30 a day. Being able to calculate your income not only gives you an idea of which sites are going to be your superstars, it's also handy for presenting data to potential customers if you decide to sell your site on Flippa.

Chapter 24: Themes & Monetization

While certain themes such as Flexibility and Thesis are good all-around themes, there are actually themes available for specific business models. Here are some popular themes for certain methods of monetization and explanations as to why they work.

AdSense Themes

When creating an AdSense site your primary goal is to get people to click on your ads, of course. One of the key factors to making this happen is ad placement. The simple fact of the matter is that ads placed in certain areas of your site get clicked on more than others. AdSense themes seek to optimize your site by placing ads in these locations to ensure that you're getting as many clicks as possible.

Popular AdSense Themes:

- Heatmap Reloaded
  http://www.top-adsense-themes.com/wordpress-adsense-themes/heatmap-reloaded-adsense-ready-theme/
- Clearness
  http://www.top-adsense-themes.com/Clearness
- Mono Sense
  http://www.top-adsense-themes.com/MonoSense
- Ads Minded
  http://www.sapiensbryan.com/ads-minded-wordpress-theme/index.php/archives/ads-minded-wordpress-theme/

Landing Page Themes

If you're selling your own products you want to make sure you have a good landing page set up that minimizes distractions, focuses attention on the sales copy, and presents a streamlined user experience that guides visitors to the buy button. Good landing page themes are simplistic, straightforward, and designed to support sales copy.

Popular Landing Page Themes:

WP Sales Letter Theme
http://wp-saleslettertheme.com/

Sales Lead
http://thinkdesignblog.com/free-wordpress-theme-saleslead-make-product-sales-pages-fast.htm

Blogging Themes

If you want to make money blogging you need a sleek and modern theme to provide an exceptional user experience to your visitors. This is often referred to as Web 2.0. Because blogs can be monetized in a variety of ways, and often end up incorporating more than one method, you have a lot of options. A good blogging theme presents easy navigation, attractive graphics, and intelligent sidebar setup.

Popular Blogging Themes:

Evolution
http://www.elegantthemes.com/gallery/evolution/
Modernize
http://themeforest.net/item/modernize-flexibility-of-wordpress/1264247
Aware
http://themeforest.net/item/modernize-flexibility-of-wordpress/1264247
Reaction
http://themeforest.net/item/reaction-wp-responsive-rugged-bold/702169

Bloggin Pro
http://www.bloggingpro.com/archives/2007/03/21/blogging-pros-theme-released/
Mimbo
http://www.darrenhoyt.com/2007/08/05/wordpress-magazine-theme-released/
Digital Pop
http://www.writerspace.net/index.php/2007/04/01/digital-pop-wordpress-theme/

Product Review Themes

Selling products from Amazon.com review site, or other online affiliate programs, is always a lot easier when you have a theme designed specifically for that purpose. These themes make sure that the products take center stage and that ratings, customer reviews, and other important information are easily visible to viewers. In many cases these themes are very image oriented, especially on the main page, allowing visitors to navigate to the products of their choice quickly and easily.

Popular Product Review Themes:

- ProReview Theme
  http://proreviewtheme.com/
- Theme Simple for Amazon Store
  http://wppoint.com/themes/theme-simple-for-amazon-store.html
- WP-Clear
  http://www.solostream.com/wordpress-themes/
- Zenko
  http://www.wpzoom.com/themes/zenko/
- Arras
  http://www.arrastheme.com/

Digital Product/EBook Sales Themes

For sites that specialize in selling digital products, you want a theme that emphasizes the products visually. Relatively large pictures, sidebar images, and a clean design are musts.

Popular Digital Product/EBook Sales Themes:

- ⚔ eProduct by Templatic
  http://templatic.com/news/eproduct/
- ⚔ eBook by Templatic
  http://templatic.com/cms-themes/ebook/
- ⚔ MyProduct theme by ElegantThemes
  http://www.elegantthemes.com/gallery/myproduct/

Directory Website Themes

If your website is a directory, your main emphasis needs to be ease of navigation. Themes that offer muti-variable searches ensure that visitors are able to find what they need fast and easy. The design should also be clutter free and present information concisely.

Popular Directory Website Themes:

- ⚔ PremiumPress Classified
  http://www.premiumpress.com/classifiedstheme/
- ⚔ eList Elegant Theme
  http://www.elegantthemes.com/blog/theme-releases/new-theme-elist
- ⚔ DirectoryPress
  http://directorypress.net/

Article Directory Themes

The main difference between this type of theme and one for a regular directory is that article directory themes are much more text oriented. This makes a simple design the best because it's easy to drown your visitor in a swamp of text if you're not careful. Themes that allow you to separate many different categories and provide easy navigation are the best.

Popular Article Directory Themes:

- Article Directory Theme by Templatic
  http://templatic.com/cms-themes/articledirectory/
- Article Directory WordPress Theme by Articlesss
  http://articlesss.com/article-directory-wordpress-theme/
- Article Directory WordPress by DailyWP
  http://www.dailywp.com/article-directory-theme/

Magazine/News Themes

These themes provide a healthy balance between text content and image content on the main page. These themes usually separate different posts into blocks and offer thumbnail images to attract attention to each section. In many cases they also have a prominent header on the main page, sometimes in the form of a carousel that rotates different featured posts. A good magazine/news theme presents a balanced view of image and text and makes navigation easy and intuitive.

Popular Magazine/News Themes:

- News Theme by StudioPress
  http://www.studiopress.com/themes/news
- Magazine Theme by StudioPress
  http://www.studiopress.com/themes/magazine
- Bold News by WooThemes
  http://www.woothemes.com/2011/01/boldnews/

Chapter 25: Being an Authority in Your Niche

When you're seeking to monetize a website you want to make sure that you are presenting yourself as an expert in your niche. This is a fundamental aspect of branding, and branding is more often than not what separates the mediocre from the superstars. For example, Nike and McDonald's are considered to be at the top of their industries although (arguably) their products aren't significantly better than their competition.

The reason they're at the top is because they focus on aggressively marketing themselves as the top authorities in their industries. To reach the top you will have to aggressively market yourself as an authority figure in your niche as well. We'll go over some of the factors you need to take into consideration in order to make this happen.

Understanding Your Niche

When you choose a niche, it should either be something you are interested in personally or something you can virtually master in a very short amount of time. To be an authority in your niche you have to be legitimately knowledgeable about it. If you're just faking knowledge and expertise, people will catch on very quickly.

One of the ways to become an authority in a niche that you're new to is to read books by people who are considered experts in the niche. When I say "experts" I mean people who have firsthand experience, if possible. Taking in this firsthand knowledge is the next best thing to having real-life experience with your niche topic.

Remember that speed is the key here. The more complicated your niche, the longer it will take to become an expert. You want something that you can learn the ins and outs of as quickly as possible.

Starting a Blog

If your WordPress site itself isn't going to be a blog, you should consider creating a separate site to function as a blog. It can be another WordPress.org site or simply a WordPress.com or Blogger.com site if you're not actually selling anything on it. Overall I would recommend WordPress.org because you will have more control over the content you post on the site.

The benefit of having a blog is that it helps people get to know you better. It is a well-known fact that people will more readily purchase things from those they know and trust. By giving them an insight into your personal life, people will develop that bond of trust with you, and you can use that to enhance your marketing efforts.

Public Speaking

This is a technique that Timothy Ferriss, author of *The 4-Hour Workweek*, developed that is incredibly effective, if you're willing to come out of your shell a bit. Basically this entails you contacting several nearby universities and offering to give a free 1- to 3-hour seminar about your niche. The more well-known the universities are, the better, and because you're doing it for free, you drastically increase the likelihood of being approved.

Once this is done you now have some notoriety and can use this to enhance your expert status online, but you can also take things one step further. By promoting the fact that you've spoken about your niche at universities, you can convince well-known, big companies such as AT&T, IBM, and others to allow you to give free presentations to them as well. Of course, what companies you contact depends on what your niche is, but the fact that you're offering free presentation and have already done presentations at well-known universities drastically increases your chances of being accepted.

With all these speaking engagements under your belt, you'll have drastically built up your credibility in your niche in a relatively short amount of time. This is one of the fastest techniques for reaching expert status, if you're willing to go through with it.

Join Trade Organizations

If there are trade organizations associated with your niche, you should consider joining a few of them. This will allow you to borrow their authority and make yourself look like more of an expert. In some cases trade organizations will require you to meet certain requirements to be able to join. In other cases you will simply have to pay a membership fee and you'll be accepted.

To find these organization just do a few Google searches and see what turns up. You can also ask others in your niche if they know of any.

Getting the Attention of the Media

Another great way to increase your credibility and establish yourself as an authority in your niche is to get in contact with the media. This can be accomplished in many different ways, but one of the most effective is to create press releases and distribute them via the right channels. Distribution services include PressMethod.com, NewswireToday.com, and many others.

http://www.pressmethod.com/
http://www.newswiretoday.com/index.php
http://socialrealist.com/digital-pr/big-list-of-free-press-release-distribution-sites/

When you write a press release write it with the intent of catching the eye of someone in the media. Make it interesting, and above all else, newsworthy. In most cases if you do get noticed, it will be by someone on a lower-tier media outlet, such as a local radio station, newspaper, or perhaps a local news station.

You can then foster connections with these media outlets to work your way up the chain to more prestigious outlets.

In some cases it can be worth it to contact the media directly. This usually works best if you have already done the speaking presentations that we just discussed, because that will give you a boost of credibility. If you're going to do it this way, you have to be prepared to be turned down before you find someone willing to give you the time of day.

NOTE: You can outsource press release writing. Check the Resources section.

Write for a Trade Magazine

If there is a magazine that is closely related to your niche, offer to write an article for them. If they decline you can try offering to interview an expert in that niche instead. The beauty of this is that even if you do just conduct an interview, you will still be listed as a contributor to that magazine and gain credibility.

Make Connections

One of the best ways to ensure that you're viewed as an authority in your niche is to make friends with others that are considered authority figures in your niche. Once again this allows you to borrow the credibility of others and use it for yourself.

The key to doing this successfully is to be able to prove that you have something to bring to the table and show them that you are worth being friends with. If you're a complete newbie in your niche, and have nothing to show for it, most authority figures in your niche probably won't take you seriously. In most cases you should work on getting some experience and credibility under your belt before you try to make these connections. However, there may be situations in which you can convince one of these experts to take you under their wing if you can show that you have potential.

Credibility = Money

In the end, the amount of credibility you have will likely directly impact the amount of money you make. If you become a well-known powerhouse in your niche people will flock to you and practically throw their money into your bank account, as long as you offer them quality products and services. This also makes getting traffic much easier because you will be able to take advantage of word of mouth.

Day 6 Recap

Here is what we went over today.

- The different ways you can monetize your website
- How some monetization methods can be combined
- Why you should always be testing your monetization efforts
- How to find your target audience and why it is important
- Why targeted traffic is important
- Several different methods of driving traffic
- The importance of backlinks
- How to match your theme to your monetization method
- How to become an authority figure in your niche
- Why building your reputation and credibility is important

Some of the things we went over today can be done immediately, such as trying out different themes, while others are going to take time. Building up your credibility, creating backlinks, and finding the best monetization method for your site through testing aren't things that you can do overnight. These tasks take patience and discipline in order to achieve and see positive results from them.

The real challenge in today's lessons will be not getting discouraged when undertaking the long-term tasks, because it can be easy to get frustrated and give up when you don't see immediate results. What is going to enable you to be successful is your ability to stick with your business model, continue testing, tweaking, and perfecting it, and learning from both your successes and your mistakes.

Remember, there are no failures when it comes to online business, only learning experiences.

Day 7: Analytics

At this point you should not only have a fully functional WordPress site set up with a theme that is conducive to your preferred monetization method, but also an idea of how you are going to drive traffic to your website. Once the traffic starts to flow, it is imperative that you have the capability to analyze that traffic and tweak your website accordingly.

Chapter 26: Installing and Understanding Analytics

Installing Google Analytics

There are a variety of ways to put analytics on your website, but the easiest is going to be to install the Google Analytics. The first step is easy, you head over to www.google.com/analytics and sign up. http://www.google.com/analytics Once you're in your account you'll start by creating a new profile for your website. You do this by clicking on the Admin button then clicking on New Account. You'll then fill out some information, and your new profile will be added.

Once your account is created click on your username and you will be taken to a screen that shows all of the websites you have added to it. If you want to add another site, click New Property.

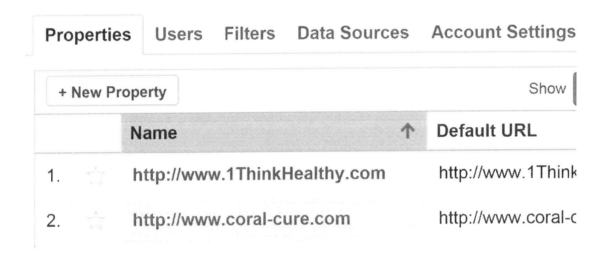

To get the tracking code you need to click on the website you want to get it for and then click the tab that says "Tracking Code." This will bring up a new page with several things on it. Scroll down and get the code where it says "Paste this code on your site."

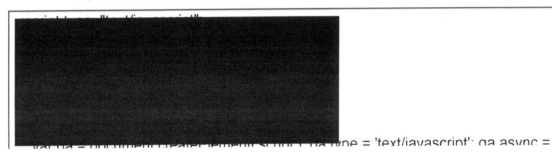

Copy that code and then go into your WordPress account and click on Appearance, then on the "editor" link. Once you're in the editor click on "Footer (footer.php)" which will be on the right side of the screen.

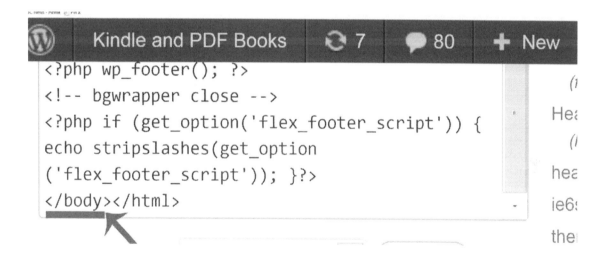

```
Author: Advantus Media, Inc.
Author URI: http://www.flexibilitytheme.com
Tags: dark, light, two-columns, custom-colors, custom-
header, theme-options, right-sidebar, threaded-comments
*/
html {margin: 0px;min-height: 100%;}.clear {clear:
both;display: block;overflow: hidden;visibility:
hidden;width: 0;height: 0;}.clearfix:after {clear:
both;content: ' ';display: block;font-size: 0;line-
height: 0;visibility: hidden;width: 0;height:
```

Comments
(comments.ph
feature.php
Footer
(footer.php)
Full Width Page
Template
(fullwidth-temp
Full Width Page

Once you're in this section scroll down in the text box until you see the tag that says </body> which should be at the very end. Paste in the code just before that tag.

```
<?php wp_footer(); ?>
<!-- bgwrapper close -->
<?php if (get_option('flex_footer_script')) {
echo stripslashes(get_option
('flex_footer_script')); }?>
</body></html>
```

Once the code is installed you can go back over to Google Analytics to view your stats. Normally it takes a day or so before the report is generated for your website.

Once you select a website on Google Analytics click on the "Standard Reporting" tab at the top to get the data from it.

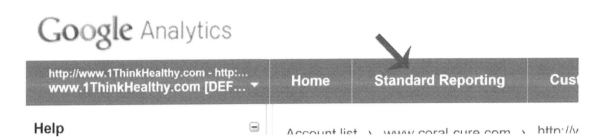

Help ⊟

Account list › www.coral-cure.com › http://v

Chapter 27: Reading Your Stats

When you take a look at your stats page you have to understand how to read your stats and know what they mean. Here is a list of all the stats displayed and what they mean.

Overview

This is a graph tracking visitors to your website. You can select the tabs that say "hourly, week, day, and month" to change how it displays. The graph is an easy way to analyze how much traffic your site is getting overall.

Visits/Unique Visits

This is simply the number of visits your website has gotten, and there can be multiple visits from a single person. Unique visits are visits by different, distinct individuals. The higher this stat is, the better.

Page Views

This stat tracks how many times pages within your site have been viewed in total. The higher this stat is, the better.

Pages/Visit

This is an indicator of how many pages your typical visitor views per visit. The higher this stat is, the better.

Avg. Time on Site

This is a measure of your visitor's time on your site total. The higher this stat is, the better.

Bounce Rate

This is a measure of how many times a visitor lands on one page then clicks off before visiting another page. The lower your bounce rate, the better.

New Visits

This measures the new visitors you get to your site. Obviously the higher this stat is, the better.

0 people visited this site

———————— Visits: 0

———————— Unique Visitors: 0

———————— Pageviews: 0

———————— Pages / Visit: 0.00

Demographics

This stat measures where your visitors are coming from and what language they speak. This can be useful if you notice that you have a lot of visitors coming from a particular area and want to focus your marketing efforts on them.

▼ Demographics

Language

Location

Site Usage   Goal Set 1

Visits ▼ | VS. | Select a m

Finding New Keywords

Something that upset many website owners late 2011 was the decision of Google to pull the feature from Analytics that monitors what keywords your visitors are using to find your site. This was a great source of new keyword ideas and allowed people to see just what keywords were the most popular for their sites. With this feature now removed, alternate methods have to be used to see which keywords your visitors are using to find your website.

There are several plugins available that are designed to perform this function. Two examples are Whassup Keywords and Hit Sniffer Live Blog Analytics. There are others for you to try out as well, and many are multifunctional.

http://wordpress.org/extend/plugins/wassup-keywords/
http://wordpress.org/extend/plugins/hit-sniffer-blog-stats/

Google Webmaster Tools
http://www.google.com/webmasters/tools
 is another source of this data. This tool allows you to see the top 1000 search keywords that people used to find your site. These stats are only provided for the

past 30 days, so you will have to manually record this data if you choose to use this tool to monitor long-term stats.

The reason finding out what keywords are being used to find your site is so important, is because it gives you a valuable insight into which keywords you should target for SEO purposes. You may find popular keywords you've never even thought of before that you can target on your site.

Chapter 28: Beating Panda

Google released their Panda update back in February 2011. This shook things up for a lot of website owners because Panda was designed to rank sites according to new algorithms. These new algorithms are used to ensure that sites providing useful, unique content and a positive user experience are ranked higher than sites that simply follow traditional SEO while offering worthless content. While traditional SEO is still important, there are other factors you must take into consideration now.

There are four main factors you need to concentrate on if you want to not only beat Panda, but use it to your advantage.

Bounce Rate

Panda frowns on a high bounce rate. To overcome this you need to ensure that your bounce rate is **less than 70%**. This means that 3 out of 10 visitors to your site need to visit more than just the page that they land on. There are several ways to encourage this.

The first way is to include a sneeze widget in the sidebar as well as a list of categories and other useful information. You can also include links to related posts in your excerpts on your main page if you have blog posts as your home page. Having these links will get more people to click through to something other than the page they landed on.

Another way to do this is to have a tab or two in the navigation bar that entices people to click on them. This can be a sneeze page such as "Hottest Topics of the Year," a page advertising a super special offer, or something really interesting. The key is to really grab your visitors' attention and get them to click on the navigation tab, then direct them further into the site.

In your posts make sure you have the breadcrumb trail that leads visitors back to the categories section and home page. This way if they land on a post they found in the search engines they can backtrack to these areas. Also make sure that at the bottom of every post you have links to related posts to encourage visitors to click through to those locations as well.

Overall getting a bounce rate of less than 70% isn't hard, but it will take some effort to implement. Just be aware of how important this stat is, and constantly be offering your viewers compelling reasons to explore other areas of your website.

Returning Visitors

This stat should be **kept above 8%,** which again, isn't hard. This is most easily achieved by offering your visitors compelling reasons to visit your site more than once, such as upcoming special offers, new releases, or other interesting events that will happen in the near future.

Another thing you should realize is that if you design a compelling site with unique, interesting information, it will encourage people to come back as well. The truth is, some topics naturally encourage repeat visitors while others don't. For example, if you create a site about the Baltimore Ravens, then Ravens fans will come back again and again as long as you offer them quality information. On the other hand, if you create a site about how to cure snoring and a person is able to purchase the cure in one visit, there is no reason for them to return later.

There are other sites you can create that encourage repeat visitors, such as sites that sell products that need to be replaced often or food items that also need to be bought multiple times. If you can offer your visitors products or a product line that necessitates that they visit multiple times, you should.

A blog can have short blurbs at the end of each blog post that give readers an idea of upcoming posts or special events. Another trick is to break up longer blog posts into multiple parts and have a "click here to read part 2" type link at the end of each post. There are a variety of ways to entice your readers to come back again and again, if you get creative.

Also, having an email list does help to facilitate this as well. You can send out alerts to your list to notify them of special offers on your site and entice many of them to visit repeatedly.

Average Page Views

This is somewhat related to bounce rate. You need to ensure that the average visitor to your site visits **at least two or more pages**. This can be tricky, but if you use the strategy I talked about earlier of incorporating sneeze page elements as well as captivating reasons to click over to other pages on your site, it isn't that hard.

Another good idea is to have a coupon page or discount page set up in the navigation bar. This will get many visitors to click on it, and once they understand how your discount or coupon system works, they'll then click to another page and use it to make a purchase or at least check out your products/prices.

If your site is a blog, try including teasers at the end of your post that promote other sections of your site. Use the elements of curiosity and big promises to your advantage.

Time on Site

To please Panda you need to ensure that the average visitor spends **at least 1:30** on your website. This may not seem like a lot, but to the practically ADD Internet generation it can be more than you'd think. Fortunately, it isn't that hard to get people to stay on your site longer than a minute and a half if you're offering them compelling content.

The key to this is offering compelling information that keeps the visitor reading. This goes back to providing useful content and a good user experience. Also, if you can continuously prompt your visitors to click links and go deeper into your site, it helps to increase the amount of time they spend on the site. This ties in with both having a low bounce rate and having multiple page views.

Another great way to get people to stay on your site for longer is to include videos in many of your posts. Videos take time to watch and can keep visitors captivated for a decent amount of time. Try including videos as often as possible on your website without overdoing it.

Social Likes

Another factor that is somewhat important to Panda is the amount of social likes you get on your web pages. Social likes are things like Facebook likes, Google +1's and other social points like this. Make sure you're using a plugin to put these buttons on your site or at least have the buttons at the end of every post you make. Optimally you should have these buttons displayed on every page in the sidebar or header/top feature.

Getting people to click on your social like buttons is best achieved by asking them to click on them. Just politely mention at the end of some of your posts that if the reader enjoyed the post, they should click the like buttons. In some cases you can offer an incentive, such as if a certain post receives a certain amount of likes you will release a free mini product for a limited time to your visitors.

Useful Content and User Experience

As you can tell, Panda is set up to weed out sites that only focus on traditional SEO and don't bother trying to offer a compelling user experience for their visitors. When you're building your site you need to always have your visitors in mind and design things so that they benefit.

Even if your site is an AdSense site, you still need to try and incorporate these factors into your overall design so that the four main statistical requirements are met. This does make it a bit harder to create AdSense sites than it used to be, but ranking high in the search engines will reward you with more traffic, which will in turn help you earn more money.

In the end, there really is no downside to configuring your site so that your visitors get the most enjoyment out of it. They will stay on your site longer, be less likely to "bounce" off of it, and be more likely to hit the various like buttons you have installed. Give your visitors what they want, and they in turn will give you what you want.

Day 7 Recap

What we went over today.

- How to install Google Analytics on your website
- What the different stats on Google Analytics mean
- How to compensate for Google Analytics no longer offering keyword data
- Why it is important to gather data on which keywords visitors are using to find your site
- The four most important stats for beating Panda and using it to your advantage
- The importance of social likes

- ⚔ The importance of offering useful content and a positive user experience to your visitors

Today was your final day of training. The last step to becoming a true WordPress ninja is being able to read your analytics, understand what they mean, and use that data to optimize your WordPress site on an ongoing basis. These stats will tell you where your strengths and weaknesses lie and what you should be concentrating on to make your website truly excel.

Also of note is that while Panda did have a huge negative impact on many online marketers and bloggers, you should see this as an opportunity. You can now take advantage of a more level playing field and compete more easily against larger websites, as long as you're focusing on offering your visitors useful content and an exceptional user experience.

With the knowledge and tools you now have at your disposal, you can create incredible, and profitable, WordPress websites. All that's left now is for you to take action and make it happen!

Conclusion

This wraps up the *WordPress Domination* guide, and congratulations on making it this far. You now have an excellent set of beginner, intermediate, and advanced WordPress techniques that will allow you to not only build WordPress sites, but also monetize them and drive traffic to them.

The beauty of the WordPress platform is that it's so simple. As you get more experience you should be able to set up complete sites in less than an hour. In fact, some people are capable of doing it in less than half an hour. The point is, you can now create as many sites as you want and begin building a complete online business.

If building multiple sites isn't something that you're interested in, there are other money-making opportunities available to you now, thanks to what you've learned from this guide. Why not take your newfound WordPress mastery and sell a site-building service to others, if building sites for yourself isn't your thing?

As mentioned before, this guide was very specific in some areas while a bit more vague in others, because I can't cover how to set things up for every single hosting company, every single theme, and every single type of site you may want to create. If you ever find yourself stuck, remember that Google and YouTube are your best friends. Also, keep reading for a handy resource section that will be sure to help you with various aspects of WordPress site construction and more.

In the end, WordPress is powerful, but only as powerful as you allow it to be. To truly take advantage of this guide and become a true WordPress ninja, you have to put this knowledge into practice. If you've been following along and doing the lessons as they were taught, good for you! If not, it's never too late to get started and begin mastering the power of WordPress for fun and profit.

Until then, I wish you nothing but success on WordPress and all of your online business ventures!

Your Friend,

Lambert Klein

Resources

Hosting Services

Bluehost
http://www.bluehost.com/
HostGator
http://www.hostgator.com/
iPage
http://www.ipage.com/
Fat Cow
http://www.fatcow.com/
Inmotion Hosting
http://www.inmotionhosting.com/
host monster
http://www.hostmonster.com/
easyCGI
http://www.easycgi.com/
myhosting
http://www.myhosting.com/
Network Solutions
http://www.networksolutions.com/

Autoresponders

Aweber
http://www.aweber.com/
Imnica Mail
http://www.imnicamail.com/

Mail Chimp

http://www.mailchimp.com/

Privacy Policies

freeprivacypolicy.com

http://www.freeprivacypolicy.com/

free generic privacy policy

http://www.inixmedia.com/2010/03/free-privacy-policy-sample-template-for-a-new-website/

FTP

Filezilla   Free

http://filezilla-project.org/

CuteFTP   (This one costs from $25 to $60)

http://www.cuteftp.com/

Press Release Services

List of 50 Free Press Release Services

http://www.avangate.com/company/resources/article/press-release-distribution.htm

Themes

News/Magazine:

News Theme by StudioPress

http://www.studiopress.com/themes/news

Magazine Theme by StudioPress

http://www.studiopress.com/themes/magazine

Bold News by WooThemes
http://www.woothemes.com/2011/01/boldnews/

Article Directory:
Article Directory Theme by Templatic
http://templatic.com/cms-themes/articledirectory/
Article Directory WordPress Theme by Articlesss
http://articlesss.com/article-directory-wordpress-theme/
Article Directory WordPress by DailyWP
http://www.dailywp.com/article-directory-theme/

Directory:
PremiumPress Classified
http://www.premiumpress.com/classifiedstheme/
eList Elegant Theme
http://www.elegantthemes.com/blog/theme-releases/new-theme-elist
DirectoryPress
http://directorypress.net/

EBook/Product:
eProduct by Templatic
http://templatic.com/news/eproduct/
eBook by Templatic
http://templatic.com/cms-themes/ebook/
MyProduct theme by ElegantThemes
http://templatic.com/cms-themes/ebook/

Product Review/Affiliate:
ProReview Theme
http://proreviewtheme.com/
Theme Simple for Amazon Store
http://wppoint.com/themes/theme-simple-for-amazon-store.html

WP-Clear

http://www.solostream.com/wordpress-themes/

Zenko

http://www.wpzoom.com/themes/zenko/

Arras

http://www.arrastheme.com/

Blogging:

Evolution

http://www.elegantthemes.com/gallery/evolution/

Modernize

http://themeforest.net/item/modernize-flexibility-of-wordpress/1264247

Aware

http://themeforest.net/item/modernize-flexibility-of-wordpress/1264247

Reaction

http://themeforest.net/item/reaction-wp-responsive-rugged-bold/702169

Bloggin Pro

http://www.bloggingpro.com/archives/2007/03/21/blogging-pros-theme-released/

Mimbo

http://www.darrenhoyt.com/2007/08/05/wordpress-magazine-theme-released/

Digital Pop

http://www.writerspace.net/index.php/2007/04/01/digital-pop-wordpress-theme/

Landing Page/Sales Page:

WP Sales Letter Theme

http://wp-saleslettertheme.com/

Sales Lead

http://thinkdesignblog.com/free-wordpress-theme-saleslead-make-product-sales-pages-fast.htm

AdSense:

Heatmap Reloaded

http://www.top-adsense-themes.com/wordpress-adsense-themes/heatmap-reloaded-adsense-ready-theme/

Clearness

http://www.top-adsense-themes.com/Clearness

Mono Sense

http://www.top-adsense-themes.com/MonoSense

Ads Minded

http://www.sapiensbryan.com/ads-minded-wordpress-theme/index.php/archives/ads-minded-wordpress-theme/

Squeeze Page:

Flex Squeeze

http://www.flexsqueeze.com/flexsqueeze/

General:

Flexibility

http://www.flexibilitytheme.com/

Thesis

http://diythemes.com/

Domain Registrars

Go Daddy

http://www.godaddy.com/

Namecheap

http://www.namecheap.com/

Enom.com

http://www.enom.com/

Moniker

http://www.moniker.com/

Reseller Club

http://www.resellerclub.com/products/domain-registration

MelbournIT

http://www.melbourneit.com.au/

Network Solutions

http://www.networksolutions.com/

MyDomain

http://www.mydomain.com/

Plugins

Zemanta

http://www.zemanta.com/

Automatic SEO Links

http://wordpress.org/extend/plugins/automatic-seo-links/

SEO Friendly Images

http://wordpress.org/extend/plugins/seo-image/

SEO Tag Cloud Widget

http://wordpress.org/extend/plugins/seo-tag-cloud/

SEO Title Tag

http://wordpress.org/extend/plugins/seo-title-tag/

Slick Social Share Buttons

http://wordpress.org/extend/plugins/slick-social-share-buttons/

Subscribe to Comments

http://wordpress.org/extend/plugins/subscribe-to-comments/

Personal Favicon

http://wordpress.org/extend/plugins/personal-favicon/

SEO Ranker Report

http://wordpress.org/extend/plugins/seo-rank-reporter/

WP-PageNavi

http://wordpress.org/extend/plugins/wp-pagenavi/

Google Analyticator

http://wordpress.org/extend/plugins/google-analyticator/

Breadcrumb NavXT

http://wordpress.org/extend/plugins/breadcrumb-navxt/

WordPress Related Posts

http://wordpress.org/extend/plugins/wordpress-23-related-posts-plugin/

WP Super Cache

http://wordpress.org/extend/plugins/wp-super-cache/

Google XML Sitemaps

http://wordpress.org/extend/plugins/google-sitemap-generator/

All in One SEO Pack

http://wordpress.org/extend/plugins/all-in-one-seo-pack/

Contact Form 7

http://wordpress.org/extend/plugins/contact-form-7/

Really Simple Captcha

http://wordpress.org/extend/plugins/really-simple-captcha/

Akismet

http://wordpress.org/extend/plugins/akismet/

Hit Sniffer Live Blog Analytics

http://wordpress.org/extend/plugins/hit-sniffer-blog-stats/

Wassup Keywords

http://wordpress.org/extend/plugins/wassup-keywords/

HTML5 Video Player

http://wordpress.org/extend/plugins/secure-html5-video-player/

WP Forum Server

http://wordpress.org/extend/plugins/forum-server/

bbPress

http://bbpress.org/

Simple:Press

http://simple-press.com/

Online Backup for WordPress

http://wordpress.org/extend/plugins/wponlinebackup/

EZPZ One Click Backup

http://wordpress.org/extend/plugins/ezpz-one-click-backup/

WordPress Firewall 2

http://wordpress.org/extend/plugins/wordpress-firewall-2/

cloudsafe365_for_Wordpress

http://www.cloudsafe365.com/how-it-works/

Exclude Pages

http://wordpress.org/extend/plugins/exclude-pages/

PC Hide Pages

http://wordpress.org/extend/plugins/pc-hide-pages/

Tools

Google Webmaster Tools

http://www.google.com/webmasters/tools

Google Analytics

http://www.google.com/analytics

Article Bot

http://www.articlebot.org/

Article Submission Helper

http://www.articlesubmissionhelper.com/

OnlyWire

http://onlywire.com/

Other Social Bookmarking Software

http://www.internetgeeks.org/tech/top-automated-social-bookmarking-software-tools/

SEOmoz

http://www.seomoz.org/seo-toolbar

colorschemedesigner.com
http://www.colorschemedesigner.com/

Article Directories

List of 50 Article Directories
http://www.vretoolbar.com/articles/directories.php

Misc.

Fiverr
http://www.fiverr.com/
Copyblogger
http://www.copyblogger.com/

Tutorial Videos

SQL Database and WP-Config Tutorial
http://www.youtube.com/watch?v=snijbmA0qnY

WordPress Installation on HostGator
http://www.youtube.com/watch?v=3B_k1KqW0Dg

WordPress Installation on Bluehost
http://www.youtube.com/watch?v=uqdWyVpR6HI

Filezilla Tutorial
http://www.youtube.com/watch?v=yr_u2iKfAt0

Registering a Domain Name with Go Daddy
http://www.youtube.com/watch?v=nhtlyNgHPDg

Registering a Domain Name with Name Cheap
http://www.youtube.com/watch?v=JewCEUZrQv8

Installing WordPress Plugins
http://www.youtube.com/watch?v=BLeAv5GWG2Q

About the Author

Lambert Klein is that inspirational older brother you wish you had; that guy who knows all the ways to be successful at online marketing and is willing to share his secrets with you.

After leaving his job in construction, Lambert was determined to learn about Internet marketing. He successfully reinvented himself into an authentic and dedicated writer focusing on Internet solutions and Internet marketing.

He started out writing for other people and soon realized that he could work on his own projects exclusively to produce a generous income.

His uncompromising passion to write quality content has driven his four websites to be wildly successful.

He found that the people around him were constantly coming to him for advice on Internet marketing. That was the moment he knew that he would begin writing books about Internet solutions.

Lambert has authored several PDF reports and eBooks, as well as various Kindle books covering subjects such as blogging, search engine optimization (SEO), weight loss, and natural anti-aging.

He's most proud of the response to his most popular book on Amazon Kindle called *WordPress Power Guide*.

Lambert calls Marion Township home, where he lives on 7 acres of beautiful Michigan countryside. There you will find him hiking with his wife Lynn or strumming on his guitar.

On the weekends he enjoys heading to the ball field to take in a Tigers baseball game, playing with his cat Mitts, or enjoying a double scoop of chocolate ice cream.

It's said that you should find someone you want to be like and copy them. Lambert Klein is that guy. He knows Internet marketing, he's making money, and he's willing to share his knowledge with you.

You can contact Lambert here: http://www.lambertklein.com/

Other Books

The Power of Kindle Books: Selling and Marketing Your EBooks for Residual Income
http://www.amazon.com/dp/B007FXHKG2

Complete list of books on Amazon
http://www.amazon.com/Lambert-Klein/e/B004CK98DY/

20042806R00146

Made in the USA
Lexington, KY
17 January 2013